Praise for *The Little Blue Book*

"This book is a game changer, one that will enable Democrats to regain their language and to stop mimicking Republican ideas and rhetoric."

—Diane Ravitch, author of *The Death and Life of the Great American School System: How Testing and Choice Are Undermining Education*

"Republicans offer values. Democrats offer policies. Guess what? Values often win, even when the policies are more popular. It's about time Democrats learned how to talk (and think) in terms of the underlying values that make them Democrats—values that are more widely shared by Americans than the values Republicans espouse. Here's the essential handbook for thinking and talking Democratic—must reading not only for every Democrat but for every responsible citizen."

—Robert B. Reich, Chancellor's Professor of Public Policy, University of California, Berkeley, and author of *Beyond Outrage*

"George Lakoff is the progressive movement's Jedi master of language. *The Little Blue Book* tells us how to say what we need to say to bring about the policy changes Americans need."

—Van Jones, author of *Rebuild the Dream*

"I've always learned a lot from Lakoff, and you will too."

—George Soros

"If you only preach to the choir, you've no need for *The Little Blue Book*. But if you want to reach people you don't agree with, read this book!"

—Joan Blades, founder of Moveon.org

"George Lakoff's willingness to share his unmatched understanding of the way language impacts politics is a precious gift to his fellow progressives. In this election year, *The Little Blue Book* is a must-read."

—Bob Edgar, president, Common Cause

"Blending insight and rigor, Lakoff and Wehling have produced a Rosetta Stone that translates progressive ideas into fundamental human values that will resonate with Americans of all backgrounds and beliefs."

—Michael Brune, executive director, Sierra Club

"With *The Little Blue Book,* Lakoff and Wehling are giving Democrats and progressives a gift—the tools to inspire Americans by using the moral language of our Democratic values of caring for each other and building and protecting our community. Our leaders, Obama included, must stop falling into right-wing traps and repeating their language and frames. Our vision is far better than the right wing's. Use this book and learn from Lakoff and Wehling how we can best communicate for a future we all deserve and need."

—Don Hazen, executive editor, AlterNet.org

"*The Little Blue Book* gives progressives not just invaluable tools but, more important, an infusion of the hope desperately needed to fix our broken politics. By mapping the political brain, Lakoff and Wehling have shown Democrats the surest way to find their spines."

—Ken Cook, president, Environmental Working Group

ALSO BY GEORGE LAKOFF

Don't Think of an Elephant!
Know Your Values and Frame the Debate

The Political Mind: A Cognitive Scientist's Guide
to Your Brain and Its Politics

Moral Politics:
How Liberals and Conservatives Think

Metaphors We Live By

Philosophy in the Flesh: The Embodied Mind
and Its Challenge to Western Thought

Women, Fire, and Dangerous Things:
What Categories Reveal About the Mind

THE
LITTLE BLUE BOOK

*The Essential Guide
to Thinking and Talking Democratic*

✷ ✷ ✷ ✷

GEORGE LAKOFF
and
ELISABETH WEHLING

FREE PRESS
New York   London   Toronto   Sydney   New Delhi

FREE PRESS
A Division of Simon & Schuster, Inc.
1230 Avenue of the Americas
New York, NY 10020

First Free Press trade paperback edition June 2012

FREE PRESS and colophon are trademarks of Simon & Schuster, Inc.

For information about special discounts for bulk purchases,
please contact Simon & Schuster Special Sales
at 1-866-506-1949 or business@simonandschuster.com.

The Simon & Schuster Speakers Bureau can bring authors to your live event.
For more information or to book an event, contact the Simon & Schuster Speakers Bureau
at 1-866-248-3049 or visit our website at www.simonspeakers.com.

DESIGNED BY ERICH HOBBING

Manufactured in the United States of America

1   3   5   7   9   10   8   6   4   2

Library of Congress Cataloging-in-Publication Data
Lakoff, George.
The little blue book: the essential guide to thinking and talking
Democratic/George Lakoff and Elisabeth Wehling.
p. cm.
Includes bibliographical references.
1. Democratic Party (U.S.) 2. Elections—United States. I. Wehling,
Elisabeth. II. Title.
JK2316.L35 2012
324.2736—dc23
2012016672

ISBN 978-1-4767-0001-4
ISBN 978-1-4767-0003-8 (ebook)

To Kathleen
and
to Uta and Gerd

CONTENTS

CONTENTS

THE
LITTLE BLUE BOOK

A NOTE ABOUT THIS BOOK

This is a handbook for Democrats, intended for immediate use in the current political moment. But our discussion goes beyond polls and focus groups and the opinions of pundits: it is based on science and requires some, though not all that much, scientific background.

What people say and how they act depends on how they think. Political pundits have access to language and to actions, but they don't have access to thought. This often leads to superficial or mistaken analyses of what the public thinks and what will change public opinion. The cognitive and brain sciences have shown that most thought—as much as 98 percent—is unconscious.[1] There is a lot going on in our brains that we don't have direct access to, but what is hidden from us determines a great deal of what makes sense to us and how we reason.[2] Real reason, the unconscious kind, uses a logic very different from that typically taught in departments of political science, economics, law, and public policy. Democrats, frequently trained in those fields, have not commonly been taught the mechanisms of real thought—the neural processes that characterize phenomena such as *cognitive frames* and *conceptual metaphors*.[3] Especially in politics, these can vary considerably between conservatives and progressives, who differ in their values and their mode of reason.

Language makes use of these deep modes of thought. In the

brain, words are defined in terms of these brain mechanisms and not simply in terms of conditions in the external world.[4] The link between words and the world goes through the brain and uses those largely unconscious mechanisms.

Most political leaders and policymakers, perhaps especially progressives and those in the Democratic Party, are not aware of this science. They have been taught, and still believe, that people are at all times consciously aware of what they think and that words are defined directly in terms of the world. They commonly believe that everyone reasons the same way and that if they just tell people the facts, most people will reason to the right conclusion. But since this is scientifically false, it keeps not happening.

Fortunately, techniques have been developed that allow us to get at important aspects of unconscious thought, and we will be making implicit use of these techniques throughout this book.

Our major point is simple. Messaging is about thinking, not just language. To get language right, you have to understand the thought it conjures up.

The Importance of Moral Frames

The central issue of our time is what kind of country America is and ought to be, that is, what system of values should govern us. First, we must understand that all politics is moral: every political leader says to us that we should do what he or she recommends because it's right, not because it's wrong or doesn't matter. And today our politics is governed by two very different views of what is right and wrong.

The progressive view, mostly in the Democratic Party, is that democracy depends on citizens caring about each other and taking responsibility both for themselves and for others. This yields a view of government with a moral mission: to protect and empower all citizens equally. The mechanism for accomplishing this mission is through what we call the Public, a system of public resources necessary for a decent private life and a robust private enterprise: roads and bridges, education, health care, communication systems, court systems, basic research, police and the military, a fair judicial system, clean water and air, safe food, parks, and much more.

Conservatives hold the opposite view: that democracy exists to provide citizens with the maximum *liberty* to pursue their self-interest with little or no commitment to the interests of others. Under this view, there should be as little of the Public as possible. Instead, as much as possible should be relegated to what we call the Private. The Private is comprised of individuals (private life), businesses owned by them (private enterprise), and institutions set up by groups of individuals (private clubs and associations). The Private is, for conservatives, a moral ideal, sacrosanct, where no government can tread, whether to help or hinder, regulate, or even monitor. No one should have to pay for anyone else. Private interests should rule, even if that means that corporate interests, the most powerful of private interests, govern our lives through a laissez-faire free market. Citizens are free to sink or swim on their own.

Each moral worldview comes with a set of issue frames. By *frames,* we mean structures of ideas that we use to understand the world. Because all *politics* is morally framed, all *policy* is also morally framed, and thus the choice of any particular policy frame is a moral choice. Americans are now faced with two sets of moral choices, each leading the nation in opposite directions. Nowhere is this clearer than in the issue of health care, so let us look at this example in some detail.

Rudolph Giuliani, in his 2008 run for the presidency, likened health care to a product, using the example of a flat-screen TV. Not everyone, he argued, deserves a flat-screen TV. If you want one, work for it and save up for it. Similarly not everyone deserves health care, but you should be free to buy it if you want it. Like a flat-screen TV, health care is in this view a *product*. If you want a product, you can make the money for it and buy it, and if you can't afford it, too bad. But if you don't want a product, no one, especially not the government, should be able to force you to buy it. That should be unconstitutional—outside the powers of the government.

The problem, of course, is that this is a metaphor. Health care is not literally a product built in a factory and transferred physically from a seller to a buyer. It cannot be crated and shipped. You cannot return defective health care and get a refund. Yet the metaphor of health care as a product survived the presidential campaign and was even adopted by the Democrats.

Giuliani introduced his TV metaphor in the spring of 2008, but after the election that fall, Barack Obama, a former professor of constitutional law, used the same metaphor while reasoning to a different conclusion. In formulating his health care act, President Obama placed the product metaphor in the context of the commerce clause of the Constitution, Article I, Section 8, which gives Congress the right to regulate commerce. If health care is a product that is bought and sold across state lines, then Congress can regulate the selling and buying of it. The Affordable Care Act is based on that metaphor and Obama's interpretation of it.

What that did was impose a frame on health care—a frame from the market economy. Notice what is not in the frame: if health care is a product, it is not a right. Providing health care is thus not a moral concern; it is an economic matter. The word *affordable* fits the economic frame, as do words like *market, purchase,* and *choice.*

Obama seemingly did not even consider a Medicare-for-all model of national health care. Medicare involves a tax, and conservatives had vowed not to raise any taxes, seeing them as the process by which the government takes people's hard-earned money and wastes it. Obama also did not think he could replace the powerful private health care industry, so he chose to work with it. Doing so, however, would require regulating it, and the most straightforward constitutional basis for congressional regulation is the commerce clause. This meant that health care had to be framed in terms of the market.

Economists have long observed that there is an economic equivalence between a tax and a required purchase. The equivalence lies in the concept of fungibility. In any business balance sheet, the loss of a credit (e.g., a tax paid) is equivalent to the gain of a debit (a purchase required). That all occurs within an economic frame, where economics is all that is considered.

Conceptually, however, a tax is normally understood in terms of a frame very different from a necessary purchase. Purchasing is in what we can call the commercial-event frame of buying and selling products, while what the government does is a credit-debit exchange and is necessarily in the taxation frame.

From a conservative perspective, nearly all taxation is governmental oppression, and therefore immoral, but *purchasing* is perfectly fine because it is based in the market, and conservatives have a moral preference for the market. Obama, hoping to avoid conservative opposition to taxation and needing a basis for regulation, chose to use the power of the commerce clause, which required the "health care is a product" metaphor. The metaphor was, as usual, taken literally.

At first, Obama favored the public option, in which the government would be seen as a business competing with other businesses and selling health care at a lower price with better offerings. Medicare, run by the government, has only a 3 percent administration cost, while most health care corporations have administrative costs between 15 and 20 percent, mostly to verify and seek grounds to deny claims. Adding in profit demands, private health care spends about 30 percent of its total budget not on care but on administration and profit. This is a large part of what makes the U.S. health care system the most expensive in the world, though far from the best. The public option did not require a large, expensive staff to administer, and possibly deny, claims, nor did it have to make a profit. The government could have used the savings from administration, profit, and advertising to cover everyone.

Crucially, however, in the public option, the metaphor of health care as a product was preserved, and conservatives objected that the public option would result in unfair competition. Given the market frame, this was a position easy to argue for, and conservatives eventually prevailed, forcing the president to abandon the public option. With the public option defeated, the president reframed. He went with a plan he took to be more favored by conservatives: the individual mandate, backed by Hilary Clinton and Mitt Romney and proposed originally by the conservative

Heritage Foundation. What the Heritage Foundation and Romney liked about the individual mandate was that it forced everyone to buy insurance, thus giving the insurance companies tens of millions more customers and more profits. This version of health care was passed into law.

Conservatives never argued against any of the law's specific provisions. For example, they never said that there should be preconditions or caps. Instead they reframed. They made a moral case against "Obamacare." (In choosing this name, they made Obama the issue, not the people and their health.) The conservative moral principles applied were freedom and life, and they had language to go with them. Freedom was imperiled by "government takeover," life by "death panels." Republicans at all levels repeated this language over and over, changed public discourse, and thus changed the minds of the electorate, especially the independents. By 2010 *Obamacare* had become a dirty word, and the most radical Republicans won their elections and took over the House with a promise to repeal it.

What the Obama administration missed was the opportunity to argue on the basis of the same moral ideals of freedom and life. Serious illness without health care takes away your liberty and threatens your life. Forcing people to live without health care is an infringement on their liberty. But the White House did not choose to frame the issue with that moral counterargument; instead they discussed technical policy details.

Conservatives, meanwhile, were arguing their values. People should not be forced to pay for other people's goods. The Public should be kept to a minimum. And the individual mandate constitutes a government takeover: if the government can force people to buy particular products, it can force them to do anything at all. Liberty is imperiled.

In all of this, the Obama administration's rationale inadvertently helped its opponents by adopting the product metaphor and placing health care in a market context.

In 2012 the Roberts Supreme Court took up the conservative frame. The conservative justices, taking the product metaphor literally, again argued that the individual mandate forces people to buy a particular product: health care. If the government can do that, it can force you to buy burial plots or cell phones or even broccoli! The government would no longer be regulating commerce but bringing it into existence. Citizens would be forced to pay for other people, thus denying individual liberty. The result would be a "government takeover."

At this writing the Court has not yet decided, but one can see where this is going. Medicare and Social Security are likely next in line, as is environmental legislation, which serves the public interest over the private and thus threatens the use of private property. At stake is the very idea of the Public. At stake is the view of democracy as a system in which citizens are bound to fellow citizens, with each individual bearing social as well as personal responsibility.

This state of affairs should never have come to pass. Health care should never have been a market issue. The Constitution gives Congress the right to "provide for the . . . general welfare of the United States." That right should have been, and should be, the moral and conceptual basis of health care law. But because it was not, because the issue was placed within a market frame, the general welfare of the United States is in danger. Do we care about each other? Are we proud that we have contributed to the liver transplants of those who need them? Are we proud to save the lives of our fellow Americans on a daily basis? Will we recognize that, without the Public, we have no reasonable private lives or private enterprise? And will we recognize that the dismantling of the Public exposes us to corporate control over our lives—not for our well-being but for corporate profit, and not under the control of a government we elect and can change but under the control of corporate managers we did not elect and cannot change?

We are writing this book because the centrality of this issue is not now in public discourse, and we hope the Democratic Party and its candidates bring it to the fore. To do so, they need to use language appropriate to the moral views they believe in.

Language is not a matter of "mere words" or wordsmithing. Words mean things. They are defined by conceptual frames. In politics those frames are morally based. They are the same morally based frames that underlie—and precede—our policies. To discuss political language is to discuss morality and policy.

This fundamental truth contradicts a long-standing myth about political communication, a myth that comes from the advertising world. The word *messaging* is defined in terms of that myth, namely, that morality and policy are independent of messaging. In this myth messaging is just wordsmithing, finding the "words that work" to sell the policy, conceptualized as a product being marketed.

There are two problems with this idea. First, communication and policy are based on the same moral frames. Policy doesn't come first, followed by communication, as the health care example shows. Second, the messaging myth is fundamentally undemocratic, placing politics in a business marketing frame, where any marketing that "sells" is sanctioned and preferred. In this view, citizens are consumers of politics, and politicians are looking for ways to "sell" them ideas. This is in direct contradiction with the Democratic understanding of how democracy should work, a view that is shared by most Americans.

Our alternative is communication based on moral and conceptual transparency. Know your values and say what you believe. Will this work? It depends on how well it is done. Moreover we believe that most Americans care about their fellow citizens. That is the moral basis of Democratic thought, and we think the public will respond to it.

Finally, a caveat. This book is not intended to be exhaustive. It's too short, and a book much bigger would probably be too long. We will cover a great deal but far from the full range of topics.

We jump in with the most pressing challenges facing Democrats and with hands-on communication advice. Next, we explore the effects, especially the hidden effects, of extreme conservatism. Third, we turn to ideas that Democrats need but that are not yet in public discourse, along with the new language needed to express those ideas. Finally, our "Phrasebook for Democrats" covers the most controversial areas in current politics, providing relevant background and introducing new ways to talk.

Our job here is to go beyond policy and punditry and the same old ideas. We hope it will change the way you see, understand, and discuss American politics.

PART I

★ ★ ★ ★

THE BASICS

1

Politics and Morals

All politics is moral. So part of the job of every political leader is to show how everyday values link to policies. This is necessary in a democracy, which depends on citizen commitment to the political process. A failure to use language linking values to policies is a failure of the democratic process.

One of the problems we see for liberal democracy is that conservatives use language more effectively than liberals in communicating their deepest values. Liberals assume their own values are universal values, and then further assume that all they need to do is present the facts and offer policies that support these universal values.

But values are not universal. Conservatives have a very different sense from liberals of what is moral, and a difference in fundamental morality is a deep difference. It is a part of your personal identity, part of who you are and what is sacred to you. A liberal will thus never persuade a thoroughgoing radical conservative, because moral differences that determine personal identity are deep, residing in brain circuitry that is long-lasting or even permanent. Luckily there are fewer thoroughgoing conservatives than you might think.

Moral Complexity

Most people are morally complex; that is, they have complex combinations of conservative and liberal moral values. So-called moderates are mostly one and partially the other. Thus moderate conservatives will use conservative values on most issues but use liberal values on others. They may support Social Security and Medicare for seniors if they care deeply about old people, or they may support public education for children if they care deeply about children and their future. So-called swing voters use both conservative and liberal moral systems and swing to one side or the other depending on what candidates or issues regularly get their attention. The same is true of many independents.

Why does moral complexity matter? Because it determines elections.

To address moral complexity, you have to understand something basic about how the brain works. Each moral system is represented in the brain by neural circuitry. A complex moral system has neural circuitry for two conflicting moralities, which are usually applied to different issues and situations. How can conflicting moralities exist in the same brain? When the brain circuit for one inhibits the other. When one is turned on, the other is turned off. You may not even notice the switch.[5]

A swing voter's conservative morality will tend to be activated by conservative language; similarly, liberal language will tend to activate a swing voter's liberal morality. The repeated use of conservative or liberal moral language is often the decisive factor in whether an independent uses a liberal or conservative moral system for a given election.

Language Is Political

Language is not neutral. Every word is defined in the brain through frame-circuits. These characterize both moral values and the particular issues that make sense only in terms of moral values. Moreover the frame-circuits are not simply logical. They are connected to emotions, governing our gut intuitions about political issues and limiting how issues—and even facts—can be understood. And they come with powerful images. This is how reason really works: through framing, metaphors, emotion, narratives, and imagery.

Frame-circuits come in hierarchies, and political frames are part of a hierarchy dominated by moral frames. Thus any political message about policy can be understood only in terms of moral values.

Before we turn to what moral values are, we should say a bit about what moral values are not.

- Moral values are not the same as policies. Policies follow from both moral premises *and* facts. Voters care primarily about moral perspective and only secondarily about specific policy details. Medicare and Social Security, for example, are policies, morally based policies to be sure, but not moral values in themselves.
- Issue areas—global warming, health care, women's rights, integration, and so on—arise from moral values, but they are not the values themselves.
- Great abstract ideas like freedom, justice, fairness, equality, and unity are also not moral values in themselves. Indeed they are each "contested concepts,"[6] with utterly different conservative and liberal versions arising from differences in moral values. If you are going to talk about these ideas, make the underlying values clear from the start.

Let us now turn to what moral values are.

2

What Are Moral Values?

Your values govern your everyday life—the decisions you make, how you treat yourself and others, and what you think about the world: about nature, business, culture, religion, family life, and so on. In American politics, your values also determine what you think democracy is.

For progressives, democracy begins with citizens caring about each other, taking responsibility both for themselves and for their fellow citizens. Individual responsibility is thus inseparable from social responsibility. The basic moral values here are empathy and responsibility, for both oneself and others.

This leads to a view of government as having certain moral obligations: providing protection and empowerment for everyone equally. This in turn requires a vibrant commitment to the Public: public infrastructure (roads, buildings, sewers), public education, public health, public parks, public transportation, public policing, an energy grid, public access to water and an adequate food supply, and the regulation of commerce. No private business and no entrepreneur can prosper without such public provisions. There is no prosperity and no sense of a civilized and decent life without these things that we have provided together. The private depends on the public.

These progressive public values commonly follow from certain ideal progressive family values, projected to larger institutions. The progressive family has parents of equal authority. Their central moral role requires empathy with each other and their children; it requires self-responsibility and responsibility for the well-being of other family members. Respect for parents comes not from fear of punishment but from admiration and a sense of cooperation. Behavioral standards and limits play a crucial role in this model. They are always subject to questioning and explanation, but parents have the last word because they are ultimately responsible. This requires open communication, transparency about family rules, shared decision making, and need-based fairness. The outcomes of family life require the cooperation of the whole family, working together as a family system. (The fact that nurturance requires standards and limits of behavior is sometimes overlooked by those who mistakenly see the openness of nurturance as indulgence and an "anything goes" attitude, which is in fact anathema to real nurturance.)

This is an idealized view. Because our first acquaintance with being governed is within our families, we come to understand ideal governing institutions (e.g., religious organizations, schools, teams, and nations) in terms of ideal families. The notion of what is *ideal* is key. You can learn about family ideals in your own family but also in the families of others and in your culture and community. Thus the issue is not just how you happen to be brought up but what you understand about how an ideal family should function.

When this idealized family is projected onto other institutions, we get nurturant versions of religions and schools, rehabilitation in prisons, a foreign policy that cares about the "family of man," and a market in which the role of business is to provide for consumers, workers, and communities as well as business owners and stockholders.

The idealized conservative family is structured around a strict father who is the natural leader of the family. Because the world is a dangerous place, and evil a force in the world, he has to be strong to protect his family. He is moral and knows right from wrong. Because children are born just doing what feels good rather than what is good, he has to teach them right from wrong by punishing them when they do wrong so they will do right in the future. Because he knows what to do, his authority is absolute and unchallengeable. He sets the rules and is, in short, the decider. Physical discipline is necessary to produce moral discipline. The enforcement of rules must be strict or they will cease to be followed. Love is tough love; discipline is a form of love. Toughness is important and a measure of moral strength. Better to discipline too often than too little. The role of the mother is to uphold the authority of the father. If she does not, she may have to be disciplined as well.

From this, certain things follow for one's outlook on society. To be prosperous, one must be fiscally disciplined. Thus if you are not prosperous, it must be because you are undisciplined—which is itself a form of immorality—and so you deserve your poverty. In this form of direct causation, effects can be traced to a single and straightforward cause.

The strict father family commonly, but not always, involves in-group nurturance. That is, spouses and children who are obedient are loved, cared for, and rewarded. When children become adults they become their own strict parents, and no outside authority should meddle in their lives.

When this idealized family model is projected onto various governing institutions, we get conservative religion with a strict father God, a view of the market as decider with no external authority over it (such as government, unions, or the courts), and strictness in other institutions, such as education, prisons, businesses, sports teams, romantic relationships, and the world community.

For conservatives, democracy is about liberty, individual responsibility, and self-reliance—the freedom to seek one's self-interest with minimal or even no commitment to the interests of others. This implies a minimal public system and a maximal private system. It is assumed that it is natural and moral to seek one's own self-interest, that it is natural to compete when there are scarce resources, that it takes discipline to succeed in a competitive world, and that there should be no interference with such a natural mode of life, especially from government. What makes society possible are laws and moral standards, which should be followed strictly. The good things in society are provided by private individuals and entrepreneurs who are seeking their own interests.

Before going further, we should emphasize what values do: **Values provide the moral premises for policy, the concern with issue areas, and the interpretation of abstract and widely shared ideas.**

Progressive and conservative value systems are thus commonly structured in terms of idealized family value systems. Policies follow from values, but they are not values themselves. Concerns about issues are not values themselves. And great abstract ideas like freedom, equality, and justice are not values. Indeed they take different forms depending on which values you have.

Take the values of discipline and self-reliance in the strict father family model. Based on those values, people who have prospered deserve their prosperity and should not be punished with taxation, nor should they have to pay taxes to support those who are not morally disciplined enough to become prosperous. Issue areas of concern to conservatives include the free market with maximal privatization, sexual morality as controlled by the strict father, harsh punishment in the courts, and a strong military.

For progressives, the values of empathy, social responsibility, and excellence lead to a concern with the issue areas of safety nets, public education, public health, and humanitarian foreign aid, with policies in those areas. Empathy for those who are not in a position to take care of themselves, together with the social responsibility to act on that empathy, lead progressives to an understanding of government that must provide adequate protection for citizens in such a position: the elderly unable to work, the disabled, the homeless, the jobless, and those afflicted by poverty. The understanding that private success always depends on public support leads to progressive taxation: the more you earn from public support, the greater your responsibility to provide for its maintenance.

Here is an example of a major policy difference following from different moral systems. Consider the issue of whether every adult should have to participate in a national health insurance system. From the progressive perspective, everyone's health and well-being depend on public provisions: clean air, clean water, a safe food supply, sewers, public support of children's athletic programs and parks, disease control, FDA food and drug monitoring, and even seat belts and traffic lights to prevent injury. The reason all these public provisions exist is that citizens in a democracy care about each other and think that a failure to prevent unnecessary suffering is immoral. It follows that people's health and well-being depend in large measure on what the public provides. Just as the financially successful owe a debt to the public, so do the healthy. As it happens, their participation in health care systems is necessary to support health care for the less fortunate. Thus there is a moral obligation for the healthy to participate in health care, as well as the pragmatic reason that you never know when you will be injured or subject to a disease.

Conservatives do not reason this way at all. From their perspective of individual, not social, responsibility, democracy gives them the liberty to maximize their self-interest without responsibility for the interests and well-being of others. Each person's suffering is his or her own concern or the concern of his or her family, closest friends, or church, synagogue, or temple. Those who do concern themselves with fellow citizens' suffering are always free to donate to private charities. From this perspective, privatization should be maximized and all of the public provisions minimized or eliminated—on moral grounds—since no one should be paying for anyone else unless he or she chooses to. From the conservative view of the market, health insurance is a *product* sold to *consumers,* of course at whatever price the market will bear. People should have to pay whatever their health and life are worth to them.

We can see why health care is such a contested issue. Progressives see the practices of private health care firms in restricting and denying care as a restriction on the human right to life. Moreover the failure to recognize the role of the Public in private success and well-being leads to a permanently privileged class that controls a hugely disproportionate amount of wealth, material resources, and political influence—against our most fundamental democratic principles. Conservatives, on the other hand, see any role of the government in the matter as an immoral imposition on liberty and individual responsibility.

At this point the distinction between moral values, on the one hand, and issue areas and policies, on the other, should be clear. Moral values are primary. They define what the issue areas are and place limits on possible policies.

What about abstract ideals such as freedom, justice, fairness, equality, loyalty, accountability, authority, sanctity, and even caring? These are what linguists call *contested concepts.* They are ideas that appear to have a very simple, generally agreed upon meaning but that actually have radically divergent meanings depending on whether they take a strict or a nurturant interpretation. In short, you cannot assume that the same word always means the same thing in both conservative and progressive uses. In general, the meanings will differ considerably.

Let's take a single example, the concept of caring. Progressive caring, as we have seen, starts with empathy and responsibility for others. Empathy thus leads to an absolute sacredness of human life, dignity, and well-being. In politics, it is carried out by a government with a strong sense of the Public—of protection and empowerment for all—which is absolutely necessary for a meaningful Private, a decent private life and prosperous private enterprise. Progressive caring is about physical, emotional, and social well-being. It includes caring about other people's happiness and self-fulfillment, which may or may not come from financial reward.

For conservatives, caring means something very different. It means providing everyone with the liberty to seek their self-interest without interference or social responsibility for others, upholding a laissez-faire free market, ensuring that crime is punished (severely), and giving everyone the opportunity to sink or swim. Conservative caring is commonly nurturance through tough love.

At this point the idea of contested concepts, and how contestations of ideal concepts arise from moral value systems, should be clear. Moral value systems are primary. They define the way that great abstract ideals are interpreted.

A Note About Progressive Religion

Conservative Christians are politically better organized than are progressive Christians, and as a result many Americans think of Christians as generally conservative. This is not the case, and so we want to say a word here about progressive Christianity.

Conservative Christianity takes the strict father moral frame and projects it onto a view of God, onto the values of religious institutions, and onto politics. In this frame, God is seen as a strict father, offering tough love, defining what is moral, and setting absolute rules. If you obey the rules, you go to Heaven; if not, you are punished forever in the fires of Hell. You are personally responsible.

Progressive Christianity sees God as a nurturant parent offering grace, which you cannot earn. Grace has all the properties of parental nurturance. It is a manifestation of God's love, given freely and unconditionally. If you are close to God and accept His grace, it fills you, nourishes you, protects you, heals you, and makes you a moral person. Being a good Christian means loving humankind unconditionally, caring and taking responsibility for the well-being of others. Because of this view, progressive Christianity has historically played a major political role in American society—in the antislavery movement, the women's suffrage movement, and the civil rights movement. This role has been lost and needs to be regained.

It is important to keep in mind the distinction between what we call *institutional morality* and *deep morality*. The former is defined in relation to religious denominations and is at the heart of the principle of separation of church and state, which holds that the rules of a particular religion cannot be imposed on the state or on citizens outside the religion, and that the state cannot determine the rules of the religious institution. This is as it should be. Deep morality, however, originates outside of and is independent of religion. Whether or not someone is religious, he or she applies deep morality to the world: to politics, the market, education, and so on. Conservatives, whether religious or not, apply strict father morality to these areas, while progressives apply nurturant morality.

The point is that progressive churches—or any religious institutions—need to know that they may organize politically without violating the separation of church and state. They may bring their deep morality but not their religious institutional values into public discourse. They may, for example, argue for national health care based on nurturant morality but may not argue for school prayer. They may organize to support gay marriage and women's rights but may not try to convert others to a particular religious viewpoint, here or abroad. They may organize support for progressive candidates but may not ask those candidates to support specifically religious policies. In fact progressive candidates and advocates for progressive causes should be speaking regularly in progressive churches, helping those churches further politically their deepest values. Progressive Christianity has enormous potential as a source of progressive political support, and that potential should be activated.

3

Is Unity Possible?

The slogan on every dollar bill, *E Pluribus Unum* (from many, one), expresses a fundamental, foundational value deep in the American psyche. There is a longing in America for unity—for agreement, for peace.

We are regularly asked whether a single unified American political worldview exists or is possible. The question is important, and it surfaces in the desire for bipartisanship and moderation that keeps arising. We can begin to see the answer in the study of contested concepts. All contested concepts center on an agreed upon core, which is real but limited. There are simple cases where everyone agrees on what freedom, equality, and fairness are. Likewise, there are simple cases on which conservatives and liberals agree. A few examples:

- Things should work. Cars should run, electricity should be brought to our homes, airplanes should be on time and not crash, cell phones should work everywhere and not drop calls, and garbage should be collected regularly.
- People should have jobs. Everyone should be able to work for a living, do well at the job, and be paid fairly.
- People should be healthy. Major disease should be kept in check, people should take care of themselves as well as possible, the effects of illness and injury should be minimized.

- There should be public order. People should obey the laws, laws should be enforced fairly and effectively, and the courts should administer justice.
- Daily life should go smoothly. Goods should be available and affordable, traffic should flow smoothly, and people should be able to go about their everyday lives without incident.
- There should be peace. There should be no invasions or terrorist attacks, no need for war, and no threat of war.

There are also certain general moral principles:

- Murder is immoral.
- Theft is immoral.
- Harming innocent people is immoral.
- Lying is immoral.

We could go on. At this level of oversimplification, Americans agree on hundreds of things throughout our society. So what is the problem?

The problem is that as soon as we get down to the nitty-gritty details, people disagree strongly. Why? Because their different moral systems specify those details in utterly different ways. And because our moral systems are so deeply tied to our individual identity, these differences matter to us immensely. In addition, remember the phenomenon of contested concepts; most people don't notice that they mean something different from what others may mean by the words *freedom, equality, justice,* and *fairness.* They assume that their contested version is *the* correct meaning of the concept. The discord we see in America today arises to a large extent because of this incorrect assumption.

Even though Americans may be in agreement on almost the full range of issues in oversimplified cases, there are always details of specific cases and implementation that lead inevitably to ferocious disagreement. What constitutes murder? Theft? Harm?

Lying? The strict and nurturant moral systems will agree in the oversimplified central cases but give different answers in more complex situations.

Consider murder. In the central oversimplified case, an innocent victim is intentionally killed in cold blood. As soon as the progressive and conservative moral systems are brought in, however, contestation arises. Take the death penalty. The criminal isn't innocent, or at least was found guilty in a trial, but is this murder by the state? Many progressives would say yes. What about collateral damage in war? Or a shooting by a police officer in the course of an armed robbery? Judgments vary, often depending on one's moral system. What becomes clear is that the central cases that we agree on are very, very limited. Most real-world cases don't fit them, and that is why our political disagreements span such a wide arc.

What we learn from the brain and cognitive sciences is that there are no concepts external to the brain and body. This includes reason itself and the concept of morality. Instead morality, like other concepts, arises from the brain and body, but often in a complex way.

Yet recognizing that moral systems are internal to human brains does not make one amoral. You can believe your moral system on moral grounds. And you can believe a different moral system to be immoral.

The concept of morality is based on well-being—the well-being of others and your own. When you see a moral worldview regularly working against the well-being of a great many people—and perhaps even humanity itself—it is reasonable to call it immoral. It has contradicted the very basis of what morality is centrally about. We do not doubt that extreme conservatives believe that they are morally correct in their political positions. But we argue that policies based on extreme conservative morality commonly harm people, thus making these policies immoral.

So what do we conclude about the possibility of unity from all this?

People who are either largely progressive or largely conservative nevertheless have some of the other's values. That is moral complexity. And where there is an overlap they are more likely to be able to compromise and to cooperate. In the absence of moral unity, such cooperation is the best we are likely to get.

4

The Political Brain: Cascades

The brain is structured in terms of what are called *cascades*. A cascade is a network of neurons that links many brain circuits. All of the linked circuits must be active at once to produce a given understanding. Simply put, the brain does not handle single ideas as separate entities: a bigger context, a logical construct within which the idea is defined, is evoked in order to grasp its meaning.[7] Cascades are central to political understanding because they characterize the logic that structures that understanding. Language triggers cascades.

As we have just seen, there is a hierarchical conceptual structure to a political cascade:

Moral values framing
General frames exemplifying those values
Specific frames using those values
Specific issues

When you mention a specific issue, all the frames and values higher up in the hierarchy are also activated. They define the moral context of the issue. Any discussion of a specific issue activates the entire cascade, strengthening *all* parts of the cascade in the brains of those hearing the arguments for the specific issue.

Here are two oversimplified examples, first a progressive case:

Moral values: Democracy requires that citizens care about each other and take both personal and social responsibility to act on that care.

General frame: Government should provide public resources to protect and empower everyone equally.

Specific frame: Government should assure affordable health care for all, including medications.

Specific issue: Government should require that health insurance plans and employers that provide health care include coverage for birth control pills.

By contrast, here is the conservative version:

Moral values: Democracy guarantees liberty to all citizens to pursue their own interests freely with limited commitment to the interests of others.

General frame: Privatization of public resources should be maximized since no one should be forced to pay for resources going to anyone else.

Specific frame: Government should have no role in health care since no one should have to pay for anyone else's health care.

Specific issue: Government should not require health insurance plans to cover or employers to pay for birth control pills.

In political thought, cascades are commonly quite complex. They may have multiple branches, each with a structure of the kind we have outlined. And they include the family value metaphors to structure economic, sexual, religious, and political values. Let us take a more detailed look at the example of the complex cascades discussed above: whether health insurance plans and employer plans should cover birth control pills. The liberal cascade that defines this issue in moral terms starts with nurturant parent family values: husbands and wives are equal. They empathize with their children, are responsible for both themselves and

30

their children, care for their children and each other, and raise their children to empathize with and care about others, to have both individual responsibility for themselves and social responsibility for others. From this basis, three strands of logic proceed. Each strand has a highest moral principle coming from nurturant morality and a subsequent sequence of frames linking that moral principle to the policy issue about birth control pills.

Strand 1:

- In the nurturant parent family, the central value is empathy for others, together with both individual and social responsibility for others in the family.
- In progressivism, empathy and both individual and social responsibility lead to a commitment to public institutions that protect and empower all.
- Empathy requires caring about the health of others. Thus the government should work for affordable health care for all.
- Since unwanted pregnancies can lead to harm for everyone involved, birth control is an essential aspect of health care.
- Thus health insurance plans should offer coverage for birth control pills.

Strand 2:

- In the nurturant parent family, husbands and wives are equal. Empathy for others leads to valuing the freedom and self-fulfillment of others. Both of those require being cared for adequately.
- In progressivism, men and women should be equal, politically and socially. Freedom and self-fulfillment are essential. Both of those require a government that provides adequate protection and empowerment for the people.
- Freedom and self-fulfillment require health. Therefore the government should be charged with assuring affordable health care, paid for with the wealth generated in the economy as a

whole. This is fair, since no one can become wealthy without protection, empowerment, and public provisions by the government.

- Since sexual freedom is an essential form of freedom, and since self-fulfillment often requires family planning, birth control is central to health and permits freedom and self-fulfillment, for both men and women. And since birth control pills are part of health care, the government should require that they be treated the same as other forms of health care.
- Therefore health insurance plans should offer coverage of birth control pills.

Strand 3:
- In the nurturant parent family, children are encouraged to follow their own interests, shape their own beliefs, and form their own identity.
- In progressivism, freedom includes freedom of religion for all individuals. No one should be able to impose his or her institutional religious beliefs on anyone else.
- Thus it would be a violation of freedom of religion for employees if an employer were to impose his or her institutional religious beliefs on employees.
- Thus employers who contribute to health care for employees should not be able to impose their religious opposition to birth control on their employees.
- Therefore employers should contribute to the provision of birth control pills to employees who need and want them.

Let us now turn to the corresponding conservative cascade. This one also has three strands forming a complex cascade with a single special case, the policy position that health insurance plans should not have to cover birth control pills. In each strand, the highest frame in the cascade comes from the strict father morality, which corresponds to a conservative moral principle. Each strand consists of a logic linking the conservative moral principles to the policy position.

Strand 1:

- In the strict father family, the father has the responsibility of providing for himself and his own family but no responsibility for others.
- In conservatism, democracy means that citizens have the liberty to seek their own interests, without any social responsibility for the interests of others. Each citizen has the individual responsibility of providing for himself and his own family, but not any social responsibility for others. One's family aside, no one should have to pay for anyone else. Public resources should be privatized as much as possible, since public institutions and services amount to paying for others.
- Corporations have the right to maximize their profits and the responsibility to maximize the profits of their stockholders.
- Government health care amounts to people paying taxes that go to pay for the health care of others.
- Paying for the birth control pills of others is paying for the health care of others.
- Therefore employers should not have to pay for the birth control pills of others.

Strand 2:

- In the strict father family, children are born without a developed moral sense. It is the responsibility of the strict father to teach them right from wrong by punishing them when they do wrong. By being physically disciplined, they develop moral discipline.
- In conservatism, birth control pills allow single women to indulge freely in sexual pleasure without the consequence of getting pregnant. Indulgence in forbidden pleasure while avoiding the consequences is immoral behavior.

- No one should have to pay for the sexual pleasure-without-consequences of others.
- Therefore no one should have to pay for anyone else's birth control pills.

Strand 3:
- In the strict father family, the father has legitimate authority over his children and has both the right and the duty to impose his moral and religious values on them.
- In conservatism, whoever has legitimate authority over any governing institution has the right and the duty to impose his institutional religious and moral values on the behavior of his underlings.
- Thus an employer with religious or moral qualms about the morality of birth control should not have to pay for birth control pills and should be able to fire employees who use them.

As this shows, the multiple strands of conservative moral logic make for an overdetermined argument for conservatives' policy position on birth control. From the perspective of the brain, arguing for this policy position automatically activates the logic of all three strands, including the inferred moral frames, within the brains of conservatives, in independents who are partially conservative, and in swing voters who may be undecided.

The frames higher up in each strand include general conservative positions, such as the conservative view of democracy and liberty, the conservative view of the market, the conservative view of religion, and the conservative view of authority and control. The argument over birth control pills is therefore not just about birth control pills, but an occasion to activate general conservative frames and moral values in the brains of voters at large.

The Use Difference

For both progressives and conservatives, cascades exist on this and other issues. The difference is that conservative cascades are activated more frequently and intensely than progressives ones, not just in the case of this policy but with regard to all policies. Conservatives are just better at this because they have a deeper understanding of the moral basis of political communication.

The case of birth control pills has been argued by liberals on the basis of women's health, but not on the basis of freedom, equality, and freedom of religion. Instead liberals have opted for the War on Women frame. The basis for this frame is the true fact that conservative policies harm women, not just in the case of birth control pills but also in cutting funds for spousal abuse and for abortion and family planning in general and by imposing unnecessary and extremely invasive vaginal procedures on women contemplating abortion.

The War on Women strategy has the advantages of uniting progressive women in a common cause and of raising money from women. But it also has disadvantages. First, it frames women as victims under attack. Second, it posits that conservatives are involved in a conscious movement to attack women, which is hard to sell except to liberals and which is probably not true for most conservatives. Third, it leaves out conservative women who see the issue of birth control pills as largely economic: Why should I pay for the birth control pills of others?

In short, instead of using cascades that serve to promote general progressive values in the minds of moderate, independent, and swing voters, Democrats are using a frame that appeals just to liberals and that does not undercut the cascades used by conservatives. By not paying sufficient attention to cascades, liberals are leaving the most effective portion of public discourse to conservatives.

Cascades work by a neural logic. But they are not logical arguments in the mathematical sense. In classical logical arguments, the negation of the conclusion negates the premises of the argument. But in cascades, the reverse may be true. Suppose someone accepts the validity of employer payment for birth control pills but hears the conservative cascade over and over. The cascade as a whole can still have the effect of strengthening the conservative arguments and moral principles. The reason has to do with a deep property of negation, one that can be seen in the title of George Lakoff's book, *Don't Think of an Elephant!* Negating a positive frame activates the positive frame. If you try not to think of an elephant you will think of an elephant.

5

Your Language

Traditional liberal discourse strategies are not consistent with the science of how reason really works. In light of this science, here are some ways those strategies could be improved.

Liberals tend to talk about policy and about facts and figures. But as we have just seen, policies make sense only as part of a morally based cascade of frames, most of which are unconscious, working in the brain behind the scenes.

Liberals love to quote conservatives and argue against them, citing real facts. This rarely works. If a conservative argues for "cutting needless spending," liberals shouldn't argue against "cutting needless spending." They should say what they believe: "The economy needs an infusion of cash to put people to work rebuilding our infrastructure and growing our economy."

Some commentators point out that conservatives vote against their economic interests. What they miss is that those conservatives are voting their *moral* interests, and they will continue to do so. Therefore liberals need to understand the difference between policy and morality and that morality beats policy. Moral discourse is thus absolutely necessary. Failing to understand this is a major reason why the Democrats lost the House in 2010.

Always Set a Moral Context for Policy

For Democrats, we recommend sincerity and transparency. Understand your values, speak them out loud, repeat them, use the facts honestly, and link facts and policies overtly to values. Do this over and over. Be coherent, so that people know what you think is right and wrong and why you hold the positions you do. Do this not just as individuals, but together as a party. The Obama administration could have done this. They too could have talked about freedom and life:

> You are *not free* if you have cancer and no health insurance. **You could die.**
> You are *not free* if you have to sell your home to pay **to keep a family member alive.**
> When health insurance plans deny you care when you need it, **they deny you liberty.**

Liberals may think these points are obvious, but they are not. They have to be articulated, over and over, if the connections that link facts and values are to get stronger.

As Democrats, we have a moral duty to communicate effectively, honestly, and transparently, to bring together our values, our major frames, facts, and policies. How can we do this? Practice creating cascades linking values to policies. Do this out loud with your friends and colleagues. Practice talking about the moral basis and general issues, as well as the specific issue, when you argue a position. Liberals who disagree on policy may share values, but they may not know it because values are too often taken for granted rather than discussed.

Liberals also need to know what to avoid. The most important practice to avoid is repeating conservative language. By repeating their language, you repeat their ideas, enabling the ideas and values behind the language to enter the brains of the public. An example comes from Public Citizen, an organization we admire. Public Citizen recently sent out material promoting single payer health care (which we agree with) by arguing against right-wing myths and lies about it. The myths and lies were listed in big, bold type:

> Single payer is **socialized medicine.**
> Single payer will **lead to rationing, like in Canada.**
> **Costs will skyrocket** under single payer.

After each came the rebuttal "Wrong," followed by a laundry list of policy truths in small, regular type.[8] In trying to counter conservative positions Public Citizen was unconsciously promoting the conservative myths and lies by repeating them in boldface and then negating them. Even worse, the principal moral message is the conservative one in boldface.

What is the alternative? Putting the moral basis and the fundamental truths in boldface. First, "single payer" is a terrible name. It doesn't tell you what the policy is about. And worse, "paying" evokes buying and selling, placing health care in an economic frame, as if health, life, and the freedom that health brings should be bought and sold. "Medicare for all" works better. So what should you say instead?

> *Everyone's **life** depends on **Medicare for all.** Health is a **life-and-death issue.***
> *Everyone's **freedom** depends on **Medicare for all.** **You're not free if you have a serious illness or accident without treatment,** which almost everyone has, sooner or later.*
> *The **cure** for a **sick America** is **Medicare for all.** Americans care about each other. That is the basis of our democracy. **Patriotism requires Medicare for all.***
> *It's just **you and your doctor** with **Medicare for all.** Your doctor*

knows you, and only the two of you can make the best deci-
sions for your health.

The point is that the best defense is a powerful offense. A basic result from cognitive science is always to put the positive first. Whatever comes first sets the frame and determines how facts are interpreted.[9] The initial framing structures the whole discourse, whether you are arguing against or for that framing.

Shooting Yourself in the Foot

Media Matters and its partner site, Political Correction, are among the most important monitors of American public discourse. Directly or indirectly, the health of public discourse depends on how well they do their job. We believe that they and other monitors of public discourse can improve. You do not have to repeat political myths and lies in boldface in order to correct them. It is important, of course, to point out who the villains are from your moral perspective, but you have to start with your own worldview in order to show *why* villains are villains.

Media Matters does not always do this. For example, consider this headline: **"CNN's Dana Loesch: Al Gore's Climate-Change Documentary Was 'The Same Level of Propaganda' as Leni Riefenstahl's Films."**[10] In quoting the opponent, Media Matters is promoting the opponent's belief, and doing so in the headline. The headline sets the frame for the rest of the discussion.

Liberal TV commentators tend to practice the same pattern. First they will recite a quote or show a film clip from a conservative, repeat the conservative claim out loud, and only then cite the facts contradicting the claim. Activists do the same. An Occupy Wall Street sign read, "Obama is not a brown-skinned anti-war socialist who gives away free health care. . . . You're thinking of Jesus." The problem is that what those reading the sign attend to are the accusations against Obama, not the negative. President Obama himself, replying to conservative health care attacks, repeatedly said, "This is *not* a government takeover," thus putting the idea of a government takeover into the minds of those who heard him.

Let us now turn to words—what words work well and why.

Say It Simply

One finding of cognitive science is that words have the most powerful effect on our minds when they are simple. The technical term is *basic level*.[11] Basic-level words tend to be short. Basic-level words are the ones children learn most easily, making up our most basic conceptual repertoire. Basic-level words are easily remembered; those messages will be best recalled that use basic-level language.

Basic-level words work well because they are easiest to process, but that is not because they are simple-minded. Quite the opposite: they are complex. Their complexity comes from the way they are connected to the body and the way our knowledge about them is integrated with basic neural mechanisms of movement and perception.

Basic-level words activate imagery in our mind; for example, the basic-level word *chair* evokes an image of a chair; the more general, or superordinate-level, word *furniture* does not evoke a specific image. Basic-level words activate motor programs in our brain as part of our speech comprehension; the word *cat*, for example, evokes motor programs that have to do with prototypical interaction with cats, such as petting them. The word *animal* activates no such motor programs. In short, basic-level concepts are the most powerful and effective in communication due to their connection to the body and the way that aspects of their meaning are integrated.

As an example of superordinate-level and basic-level wording in public discourse, consider the environmental debate. The word *environment* is an abstract category. There is no one clear image that comes to mind when hearing it; there is no complex motor planning or visual imagery activated. Contrast this with the words *forest, soil, water, air,* and *sky.* They bring clear imagery to mind. We all have seen the sky, touched water, breathed air, and walked in forests.

When you search for basic-level wording, the following checklist helps. As you consider a word, ask yourself:

- Have I seen it with my own eyes?
- Have I touched it or otherwise directly interacted with it?
- Have I smelled it or heard it?
- Can I take a pen and draw a picture of it, even a line drawing, that people would recognize?
- Can I enact it with my own body in a pantomime that people would recognize?

If none of these applies, you are probably communicating on too high a level. Your language will be less potent.

Bring It Home and Be Authentic

A final note here for those elected to office, although what we say applies to others as well. Politics is about people. Politics is about working for and representing people and concerns citizens' everyday life. Politics changes how we live, what hopes we have, what actions we can take, whether we are healthy or sick, whether our children can go to college, whether our local museum stays open, and whether the food on our dinner table is safe to eat.

The point is that while it is often important to talk about the general, we should always bring the message home and not shy away from the concrete. People want to know how policies affect their lives. The easiest way to make that understandable is by sharing real stories, about people you have met, your own family, friends, religious institution, or community. Sharing stories with a broader audience means that you have listened, that you respect them, and that their stories affect the policies you make for this country.

Say you argue for a reform that will enable seniors to receive proper health care. Maybe you know an elder community member who struggles with lack of medication and poor care. Share a few words about that person, about how her struggle makes you feel, and why cases like hers are exactly why you propose the reforms.

Say you want to make people understand what your most basic values are. Maybe you can share a story about how you learned them—from your parents, a friend, a teacher, a stranger who impressed you by showing civil courage, someone who inspired you to be the person you are. Be humane and honest. Politics is made for people, with people, and by people. Don't create an artificial distance between you and the people you represent. Share the stories that inspire you to work for this country.

To sum up:

 ➤ *Use your own language; never use your opponent's language.*
 ➤ *Be aware of what you believe and repeat it out loud over and over; never repeat ideas that you don't believe in, even if you are arguing against them.*
 ➤ *Be positive.*
 ➤ *Be authentic.*
 ➤ *Bring it home.*
 ➤ *Say it simply.*

PART II

★ ★ ★ ★

THE EPIDEMIC
OF EXTREME CONSERVATISM

6

What Is Extreme Conservatism?

Traditional American democracy has brought beauty to the world. The idea of citizens caring about each other and taking responsibility not only for themselves but also for their fellow citizens has a moral beauty. The mission of government to protect and empower all equally through the use of the Public, defined as resources for the betterment of life provided by all, is also beautiful. It has made for civilized and humane private lives and prosperous private enterprise.

Extreme conservatism is an opposite view. Its political and social implementation would be a threat to what American democracy has brought us, and it is a threat to humane government everywhere. Luckily conservatives are not, and have not always been, extreme.

Most people are morally complex, possessing some version of both conservative and progressive moral values, which apply to different issue areas. This includes moderates, many independents, and so-called swing voters, as well as people who identify themselves simply as conservative or progressive but who actually hold the opposite perspective within their moral repertoire.

For example, certain militant progressives can be authoritarian anti-authoritarians, using strict father means to nurturant ends. Certain progressive academics may be nurturant in their politics and family life but strict fathers in the classroom. There are economic conservatives who are socially progressive. Some foreign policy conservatives support progressive values in domestic policy. In short, just because someone self-identifies as conservative, liberal, or progressive on a poll doesn't mean that the person is thoroughly one or the other.

This is important to keep in mind as we go on to discuss extreme cases of conservatism. The extreme case has largely, though not entirely, taken over the Republican Party. Extreme conservative positions are now virtually required of all serious Republican candidates and of all commentators on Fox News, conservative talk radio, and other conservative media. And extreme conservatives have tilted our public discourse in an extreme conservative direction. The use of extreme conservative language activates conservative moral cascades in the brains of listeners, and as a result conservative circuitry is strengthened and liberal circuitry weakened.

What we are trying to achieve with this book is a neural alternative that is open to important truths: the central role of the Public in American life, the overwhelming power of corporations in our public life, the predatory nature of privatization, the disastrous reality of humanly caused global warming, and the powerfully negative effect of extreme conservative policies on women's lives.

Extreme conservative discourse is taken as neutral in the absence of a progressive alternative, but it is anything but neutral. It is dangerous, and it hides truths that are crucial to human well-being, not only in America but throughout the world.

We have chosen the word *epidemic* in this section's title advisedly. The effects of extreme conservative public discourse over decades, but especially within the past decade, is right now having disastrous effects. It shows up in America in the nasty political rift in Congress and in state legislatures, where moral complexity is no longer allowed. It shows up in decisions like *Citizens United,* which allowed unlimited corporate funding to enter U.S. political races. And it shows up in other legislation and court decisions, either passed or pending, that undermine the most basic aspect of American democracy: the idea of the Public as the means to carry out the care that citizens show for one another. In short, it shows up in legislation that takes away human rights and dignity, in court decisions that allow corporate takeover of public life, and in the use of corporate funds to corrupt the political process.

The spread of extreme conservatism must be stopped, and to be stopped it must be diagnosed.

7

Consequences of the Extreme
Strict Father Model

When implemented in its extreme version, the family model that serves to organize conservative thought is harmful to children. Here is what James Dobson, the dean of conservative child rearing, has to say:

> When a youngster tries this kind of stiff-necked rebellion, you had better take it out of him, and pain is a marvelous purifier. . . . It is not necessary to beat the child into submission; a little bit of pain goes a long way for a young child. However, the spanking should be of sufficient magnitude to cause the child to cry genuinely.

> Two or three stinging strokes on the legs or buttocks with a switch are usually sufficient to emphasize the point, "You must obey me."

> By learning to yield to the loving authority . . . of his parents, a child learns to submit to other forms of authority which will confront him later in his life—his teachers, school principal, police, neighbors and employers.

> Minor pain can . . . provide excellent motivation for the child. There is a muscle, lying snugly against the base of the neck. . . . When

firmly squeezed, it sends little messengers to the brain saying, "This hurts; avoid recurrence at all costs."

Real crying usually lasts two minutes or less, but may continue for five. After that point, the child is merely complaining. . . . I would require him to stop the protest crying, usually by offering him a little more of whatever caused the original tears.

Spanking is inappropriate before 15 months of age and is usually not necessary until after 18 months.

These quotes, taken from Dobson's *Dare to Discipline* and *The New Strong-Willed Child*, embody ideal strict father morality as a guide for parenting: discipline must be strong enough to break the will of the child, children must learn to obey authorities, and empathy gets in the way of parenting.

Developmental psychology shows the overwhelmingly negative effects of strict father parenting. Attachment research has shown that strict father parenting is more likely than empathetic parenting to produce sociopaths and violent criminals. Socialization research has shown that strict father parenting, called authoritarian parenting, leads to low self-esteem; to dependence on others, especially higher authorities, for moral guidance, standards, and limits; to a high level of aggressiveness; to a predisposition to hurt others; to an inability to resist harmful temptations; to fearfulness; to a lack of empathy; and to a low level of socialization. The study of spousal and child abuse shows an overwhelming correlation between abuse and strict father parenting.[12]

Although extreme conservatives may or may not themselves have had extreme strict father parenting, they use the strict father model as an ideal, as a metaphorical guide to political action in many domains: religion, economics, education, social policy, foreign policy, administrative structure, and the justice system.

The application of the metaphor leads to disastrous policies. Extreme conservatism is a thoroughgoing application of strict father morality to all areas of governance. The result is that the harm inflicted on children in the family is spread throughout our nation and the world.

8

The Four Effects
of Extreme Conservatism

Extreme conservatism inflicts its damage in multiple venues: it chips away at democracy and the Public; it poisons the human spirit; and in the world community, it contributes to human agony and damages both America's standing in the world and America's friendships with other nations. Extreme conservatism thus is not merely about abortion, the size of government, or gun control. Extreme conservatism is an all-encompassing worldview, and its adherents want to bring into its compass the lives of every citizen.

The consequence is intransigence, a refusal to compromise, a high level of aggression toward other moral views, and the ambition of total control by the ideology itself. This intransigence showed up in the 2010 House of Representatives, controlled by extreme conservatives, who have refused to compromise with President Obama. Not only does their moral system not allow compromise, but extreme conservatives believe that if this intransigence leads to a nonfunctioning government, so much the better, since that would prove that government doesn't work. And if it leads to a failure to fund ongoing social programs, so much the better, since those programs need to go.

Extreme conservatism's all-encompassing nature and ambition are usually hidden from view. Much of its work is done in think tanks, which are tasked to come up with strategic initiatives to take control of major areas of public life. They do so by choosing crucial issues where conservative Supreme Court justices or legislators can make major changes in areas that Americans previously took for granted. At the same time, conservative communication experts find language for those initiatives that seems simple and intuitive but that hides the major effect of the issue on American democracy and the Public.

Proposition 13 in California in 1978, for example, was presented as a matter of saving the homes of little old ladies whose property taxes had risen as the values of their homes went up over many years. The proposition required a two-thirds vote of city councils to raise taxes. What was hidden was that the proposition covered mostly taxes on corporate real estate, and so over thirty years later those taxes remain at 1978 levels. Also hidden was a change in the California constitution that required a two-thirds vote in both houses of the legislature to raise taxes or close loopholes. Consequently the state eventually lost the ability to raise revenues for any progressive initiative. Prop 13 decimated public education, health care, care for the disabled, and most other social programs in California.

Another example is the *Citizens United* Supreme Court decision, which was decided 5 to 4 by conservative justices. It was technically about a small issue, a nasty campaign film from 2008 attacking Hilary Clinton. Chief Justice Roberts, however, turned it into a question of whether corporations counted as "persons" with respect to free speech, where free speech is interpreted as the unlimited spending of money on political advertising. *Citizens United* allowed the formation of Super-PACs, which can collect unlimited amounts of money to spend on elections. The effect has been to give enormous power to wealthy conservatives and corporations to help elect extreme conservatives to offices at all levels.

But on the whole the changes have occurred in a large battery of small issues that add up to a major shift in the nation's ideological balance. For example, extreme conservatives seek to control women's sexuality and reproductive health by enacting what they characterize as "small" policy proposals and measures, such as outlawing sex education, defunding family planning, limiting the availability of birth control pills, removing tax credits for abortion providers, requiring parental and spousal notification of proposed abortions, refusing abortions for rape victims, eliminating abortion coverage for women who are raped during military service,[13] refusing federal funds for reproductive health services for low-income women,[14] forcing women seeking abortions to have probes inserted into their vagina for ultrasound photography,[15] forcing women to carry dead fetuses to full term,[16] and charging women who have miscarriages with murder.[17] None of these, by themselves, is about the general issue, which is control of women's sexuality and reproductive health, and so the general issue is never discussed in national public debate.

The Effect on Democracy

Democracy is not just about government; it is about all areas of life: family, religion, education, and business. When extreme strict father values are imposed, extreme conservatism comes to run institutions of all sorts, including the following:

- *Family*: As we have seen, extreme strict father parenting is often destructive and abusive. Children in such situations, if they do not rebel, often grow up reproducing authoritarian family life and imposing it in other areas of their lives. Women who are natural nurturers may have a hard time speaking up when disagreeing in important matters.
- *Religion*: Extreme forms of conservative religion, whether

Christianity, Judaism, or Islam, have authoritarian organizational structures: a charismatic pastor leading his flock, the pope and other hierarchical Catholic leaders, a charismatic rabbi in ultraorthodox Judaism, an imam in extreme conservative Islamic communities. They decide on the "correct" interpretations of religious texts and often make major community decisions that powerfully determine the lives of others. Politically they provide organization and funding for conservative political undertakings.

- *Education*: Extreme conservatism can occur in the classroom. In some states, the notion of the parental right to physical punishment is extended to teachers. In strict father classrooms, democratic discussion and decision making are limited. Teaching is spoon-feeding: students are not taught how to think critically or how to think for themselves, but are taught to recite the right answers without questioning the teacher.
- *Business*: Extreme conservatism is common in many areas of business. There is a boss, and you do what he or she tells you to do. Employees hold no voting rights in company decisions, including decisions that affect them and where they are more knowledgeable than their bosses. Unions are discouraged or forbidden.
- *Government*: When a government comes under extreme conservative control, democracy goes out the window. For example, under George W. Bush, publicly questioning presidential decisions became an unpatriotic act. Informational websites were changed to fit conservative orthodoxy. Government regulation of private industry was not funded and there were fewer regulators. The nation started a war on false premises because it fit conservative ideology. Civil liberties were suspended under the Patriot Act. Energy policy was decided in secret. And so on.

Democracy in the American tradition operates with the honestly informed consent of the governed. Discussion of alternative viewpoints is not merely tolerated but sought. Unilateral decisions made behind closed doors are appropriately perceived as undemocratic. Democracy is not alive if it does not exist throughout society. The encroachment of extreme conservatism in various domains of life is therefore a threat to democracy.

The Effect on the Public

Extreme conservatives view democracy as providing the liberty to pursue one's self-interest without commitment to the interests of others. When they speak of "small government" and "spending," they are really talking about their deep antagonism toward the Public, toward the use of government to protect and empower all citizens equally by providing public resources. This includes *all* aspects of the Public: infrastructure, education, health, the economy, and the environment. All the public resources that allow for maximizing a decent life and prosperity for all our citizens are threatened by extreme conservatism.

The Effect on the Human Spirit

By *the human spirit* we mean those positive aspects of humanity that people show toward one another: empathy, respect, generosity, connection, emotional bonding, and identifying with the other. These elements require a sense of equality and a demand for human rights and justice in all domains of life, especially social and economic justice. Extreme conservative righteousness leads to conflict, not cooperation; to fear, not hope; to aggression, not mutual respect; and to suspicion, not trust.

The Effect on the World Community

The UN Declaration of Human Rights begins as follows:

> Whereas recognition of the inherent dignity and of the equal and inalienable rights of all members of the human family is the foundation of freedom, justice and peace in the world,
>
> Whereas disregard and contempt for human rights have resulted in barbarous acts which have outraged the conscience of mankind, and the advent of a world in which human beings shall enjoy freedom of speech and belief and freedom from fear and want has been proclaimed as the highest aspiration of the common people . . . THE GENERAL ASSEMBLY proclaims THIS UNIVERSAL DECLARATION OF HUMAN RIGHTS as a common standard of achievement for all peoples and all nations. . . . [18]

Extreme conservatives want to withdraw from the United Nations because they see the United States as superior to other nations and believe that it should not be judged by them. They will not allow the United States to be subject to the World Court or allow U.S. troops to be under the control of international commanders. In many cases, extreme conservatives refuse to support humanitarian causes. Indeed they have largely been against supporting humanistic agencies like UNESCO. They have also been against the United States abiding by international treaties such as the Kyoto Protocol. And they have largely been against nuclear disarmament. This follows from the strict father model applied to the family of nations. The United States is seen as the strict father who cannot allow anyone to be a higher authority. Strict father values must guide the family as a whole, and so conservative values must guide the family of nations.

PART III

★ ★ ★ ★

IDEAS WE NEED

9

Maintaining Democracy

Just as houses fall apart if they are not maintained, so do democracy and the gifts of democracy that we barely notice and take for granted: the right to vote, public education, human rights, due process, unbiased news, clean water, clean air, national parks, safe food, good jobs, ethical banking practices, affordable mortgages, fair elections. Extreme conservatism threatens them all. The blessings of democracy cannot be taken for granted. They must be maintained, and maintaining democracy requires conceptual and linguistic maintenance.

Democrats tend to take the achievements of democracy for granted. They consider *Roe v. Wade* to be settled law. But is it? Abortion is under attack everywhere. Public education? The movements toward vouchers and charter schools and grading teachers place public schooling in jeopardy. Civil rights? The Patriot Act took many of them away. Clean water? There is a lot less of it in the age of fracking. Unbiased news? Not on Fox. Fair elections? Not after *Citizens United*.

In each case, Democrats have reacted to the specific issue. They don't look to maintain democracy, which requires thinking ahead. They don't preempt. And they don't create the language and argument forms needed in the long term to keep what we already have. Losses are noticed only after they have happened.

Extreme conservatives make their moves while Democrats

sleep. They frame public debate in their own language over the whole range of issues. And once they get the public thinking their way, they can control the media, elect their candidates, pass their legislation, and create a new status quo. Meanwhile the Democrats have failed to frame the full range of issues in terms of what American democracy has always been about. They leave a vacuum that the conservatives fill, happily and easily, with no competition. The result is what is called *hypocognition,* a lack of ideas, and it is ideas that we desperately need.

If you lack the right language, you lack the ideas that determine the public debate, that shape public opinion, and that determine elections. The most fundamental problem with finding the right language is having the right ideas. As we have just seen, the key to playing a serious role in public discourse is to be able to link your moral values to your policies.

More and more often these days conservative ideas occupy the public debate, leaving little to no room for progressives to express their beliefs and argue for their policies. This is the result of the inadequacy of progressive communication and the lack of mastery of political cascades.

Conservatives are good at this. They think about their moral values and then find issues that embody them. They come up with policies for those issues and then successfully argue for them. This is because they've done their homework. They started out by defining public issues based on what they think America should be like.

Progressives have not done this. Instead of occupying public discourse with their own moral concerns, they engage in debates that are structured by conservatism. And when it comes to public debate, one truth always holds: what is missing from public discourse is every bit as important as what is in it.

What counts as a political issue is determined by political actors, by ordinary citizens who take political action. The issue of the disparity in wealth among Americans, for example, was brought into public discourse by the citizens in the Occupy movement, who popularized the term *the 1 percent* to characterize the portion of Americans who hold 40 percent of the country's wealth.

The right wing in America has been extraordinarily successful at bringing their values, ideas, and issues into public discourse. Before Ronald Reagan, the idea that "government is the problem" was not common in public political discourse, but now it is. Conservatives have made negative public issues of abortion, public education, pensions, safety nets, evolution, and the preservation of our environment. They have done so by using reasoning based on their moral system. And to the extent that these have become issues in public political debate, the conservative moral system has been strengthened through repetition. Progressives have made the mistake of trying to reply to conservative views on these issues instead of introducing their own morality-based issues into public debate in such a way as to undercut the conservative stranglehold on our discourse.

In this part of the book we introduce issues that have not been publicly debated, issues that make sense in the progressive moral system and that challenge the very moral system underlying conservative discourse.

First, a warning. Most public discourse uses old ideas for a reason: they can be immediately understood and argued about. New ideas are not always understood immediately or welcomed. They have to be repeated over and over, preferably not by candidates for office but by grassroots organizations, bloggers, public speakers, friends of candidates, progressive journalists, even progressive comedians. Candidates can introduce new ideas, but only if there are plenty of people behind them ready to discuss those ideas publicly and repeatedly.

Even if your audience may not understand you the first time you introduce an idea, the only alternative is to be stuck using conservative discourse and thus reinforcing conservative ideas over and over in people's brains.

10

The Public

Progressives don't talk enough about the Public in general terms. American democracy is built on the ethic of citizens caring about other citizens—empathizing with each other, taking responsibility, both individual and social, for our citizenry as a whole, and creating a public government through democratic participation. Democracy's sacred mission is to protect and empower everyone equally by the provision of public resources, what we call the Public.

The Public is necessary for the Private—for decent private lives and for private enterprise that works. We all have both private and public aspects of our lives, but private life and private enterprise both require a robust Public: public roads and buildings, clean water and sewer systems, police and the courts, public education, and public health.

No one makes it on his or her own without the Public. No one who is wealthy has built all her own roads and schools, educated his own knowledgeable employees, done her own basic research, is fully protected by his own army and police, or maintained her own clean food supply. The most articulate and successful voice on this matter has been Elizabeth Warren:

> There is nobody in this country who got rich on his own. Nobody. You built a factory out there—good for you!

But I want to be clear. You moved your goods to market on the roads the rest of us paid for. You hired workers the rest of us paid to educate. You were safe in your factory because of police forces and fire forces that the rest of us paid for. You didn't have to worry that marauding bands would come and seize everything at your factory, and hire someone to protect against this, because of the work the rest of us did. Now look, you built a factory and it turned into something terrific, or a great idea—God bless. Keep a big hunk of it.

But part of the underlying social contract is you take a hunk of that and pay forward for the next kid who comes along.[19]

Democrats need to be talking nonstop about the Public as the necessary foundation of the Private. Undermining, weakening, or eliminating the Public would be a disaster for the Private as well, destroying the sanctity and safety of American private life and the basis of most businesses.

Conservatives never mention this fundamental truth of American life because it contradicts their entire moral worldview. In the strict father family model, the father is the sole support of himself and his family. He is not dependent on the empathy and responsibility of others. He is the model of individual, not social, responsibility—responsible for himself and his family but with no responsibilities to outsiders and no major dependency on them. This is the moral code he teaches his children. This is his view of liberty.

When applied to economic issues and the market, this view defines economic freedom as freedom to pursue economic interests without interference and with no responsibility for the economic well-being of those outside of the family. This, of course, obscures the deep truth that the father's well-being and that of his family is utterly dependent on what the Public provides: the most basic freedoms that come from society's overall forms of protection and empowerment.

Democrats tend to talk about individual issues: funding for this or that program, the needs of one group or another, expressing outrage over the trampling of rights of one or another sub-population. But the general issue is the Public.

The conservative drumbeat of "smaller government" needs to be undermined by an independent and prior repeating of the Public's roles in democracy and how we all rely on the Public all day, every day. "Smaller government" really means neglecting our crumbling roads and bridges, demolishing our educational system, and dismantling the magnificent structure of American business and private life. "Smaller government" really means total corporate government and the dismantling of our nation as we know it, love it, and need it to be. "Smaller government" as defined by extreme conservatives is a stranglehold on our freedoms and a serious threat to our security.

Here is what to say:
- ➤ *American democracy is built on the ethic of citizens caring about other citizens. Its **moral mission** is to **protect and empower** everyone equally by the provision of public resources.*
- ➤ *The **Public is the foundation for the Private**—for decent private lives and for private enterprise that works.*
- ➤ ***No one makes it on his or her own without the Public.** People who are wealthy haven't built their own roads and schools, educated their own knowledgeable employees, or done their own basic research, nor are they fully protected by their own army and police, and nor do they maintain their own clean food supply.*
- ➤ ***Dismantling** the Public destroys the **sanctity** and **safety** of American private life and the basis of most businesses.*
- ➤ *"Smaller government" really means **total corporate government** and the **dismantling of our nation** as we know it, love it, and need it to be.*

11

The Shift from Public
to Corporate Government

Conservatives constantly talk about limitations on state power, thus bringing the idea into public discourse. But what is not in our public discourse is the question of limitations on corporate power, which is one of the major political questions of our time.

A symptom of democracy's waning is the wildly disparate income distribution among Americans. The top 1 percent now own more than 40 percent of the country's wealth. During the economic recovery of 2010, 93 percent of the additional income created went to the top 1 percent of taxpayers; 37 percent of those additional earnings went to just the top 0.01 percent, 15,000 households with an average income of $23.8 million. Only 7 percent of the income gains went to the rest of us, the 99 percent.[20] This wealth is mainly distributed among people who run or have a lot of stock in corporations. The largest and most powerful corporations are global, not national, and do more than simply produce products and make money in the United States. Wealth disparity translates into power disparity.

Because of the Supreme Court's 5–4 *Citizens United* ruling, corporations gained extraordinary political power: the power to give unlimited money to Super-PACs, which are organizations that fund candidates in elections. Corporations are using this power to shift the governing structure of the country to themselves. They mainly (though not wholly) support conservative candidates and causes, with the goal of eliminating those aspects of the Public that do not serve corporate interests. Perhaps the most common mechanism is the manipulation of the idea of deficits.

Following the economic collapse of 2008, middle-class incomes are down, as are income tax collections. Conservative officeholders are refusing to raise taxes as a matter of conservative principle, thus creating deficits. The goal is comprehensive privatization— the replacement of elected governments with unelected corporate governments running more and more aspects of American life for their own profit, not for the public good.

Deficits are not framed as conservative creations intended to eliminate as much of the Public as possible. The metaphor that is commonly used is a version of the nation as a family and the national budget as a family budget. If a family is in debt and about to run out of money, it has to cut spending on anything that is not absolutely essential. The conservatives argue that the U.S. deficit functions just like that. But the national budget does not function like a family budget at all. First, the money owed by the federal government is mainly owed to other Americans, and only a relatively small amount is owed to foreign nations. Second, U.S. credit has not gone down: U.S. Treasury bonds are still being bought, and the federal government can borrow money very cheaply. Third, the nation can strengthen its economy through internal investment using borrowed money—say, by creating jobs in infrastructure, education, health, and research. In the long run, this is the way to strengthen the economy and get out of debt. (One should also recall that the national debt was caused by two unfinanced wars, cutting taxes to millionaires, and the removal of regulations on investment banking that led to the international financial breakdown.)

Conservatives promote the myth that the nation's debt was

caused by indulgent government spending on the Public and that the remedy is to eliminate as much of that spending as possible. This parallels the conservative myth about the mortgage crisis. The crisis had three causes, the first two due to a lack of regulation: the unscrupulous deception of prospective homeowners who were sold balloon mortgages that were incomprehensible and that they couldn't afford; the bundling of those mortgages into worthless securities that were deceptively sold to banks both here and abroad; and the refusal of conservatives to stop foreclosures with legislation. The myth is that the crisis was caused by the victims buying houses they couldn't afford. The conservative response is punishment of those victims, which helps the corporations and those who run and own them.

The corporate bailouts were made with taxpayer money, which probably forestalled a worldwide depression and which has largely been paid back. But nothing much has changed. Wall Street is operating pretty much as before, and even the mild constraints of the Dodd-Frank legislation are being fought vigorously. Wall Street income and bonuses are still huge, and banking practices have hardly changed. And all attempts to make changes have been stopped by the conservative Congress, whose election was largely financed by corporations in the wake of the *Citizens United* decision.

These matters need to be in public discussion, starting with the shift from public to corporate political power and the role of conservative ideology in that shift. The issue is the proper balance between the Public and the Corporate. Both need each other. Corporations should create goods and services that people need at a reasonable profit, without any harm. Government regulation exists to achieve this. Honest business has been the American way for a long time, supported by the Public, regulated by the government, and producing goods, services, and well-paying jobs. All in balance. We need to get back to that.

Here is what to say:

➤ *Privatization is the **replacement of elected governments with unelected corporate governments**, which run more and more aspects of American life **for their own profit, not for the public good**.*

➤ ***Wealth disparity is power disparity. Extreme wealth results in political power that ordinary citizens don't have.***

➤ *As more of the Public is **eliminated and privatized**, corporations make more money, though ordinary people do not. Moreover ordinary people lose what the Public gives them: the means for a decent life.*

➤ *Corporations have extraordinary political power, the power to give unlimited money to organizations that fund candidates in elections. This power is being used by corporations to **shift the governing structure** of the country to themselves. This is **undemocratic**.*

➤ *Conservative officeholders who refuse to raise taxes as a matter of conservative principle are **creating deficits**.*

➤ *The Public and the Corporate **need each other and need to be in balance**. Honest business has been the American way for a long time, supported by the Public, regulated by the government, and producing goods, services, and well-paying jobs for citizens.*

12

Corporations Govern Your Life

There is a liberal version of the free market that overlaps with the conservative version. In the liberal version, the free market functions for the betterment of the nation and all of its citizens, giving us the products we need at a reasonable cost with a reasonable profit, creating innovative and useful products through pure competition, customer service, complete transparency, accountability to customers, workers rights, and living wages. That is the liberal ideal, and it is sometimes met. This is the kind of corporation we commonly see in corporate advertising. But it's not the whole truth. The truth is that corporations govern our lives often in ways that rarely enter public discourse. They do so in ways that are intrusive, oppressive, and even tyrannical. Here are some examples:

- Health insurance companies determine what kind and level of care you get and at what cost. They therefore have considerable control over your health and your life, yet you are not involved in the decisions they make about your health and life.
- Agricultural and food corporations govern access to healthy food and determine, for many people, what is available to eat and what is in it: pesticides, antibiotics, hormones, trans fats, corn syrup, mercury, and unhealthy chemicals.
- Media corporations determine, to a considerable extent, what

news you get and how it is framed and therefore shape how your brain will be constrained in understanding the world. This is a form of corporate brain control, which in turn has consequences for political control.

- Corporations also govern what culture we have access to: what movies are made, what is shown on TV, what music is released, and what art is made widely accessible.
- Corporations govern how we communicate and get information, for example, through exclusive high-priced and long-term cell phone contracts.
- Through planned obsolescence of, for example, electronic equipment, cars, and household appliances, corporations govern how much money we have to spend on maintaining the basics of modern life.
- Corporations intrude on our personal lives by collecting private information about us, snooping on the way we use our computers, calling us at home, and filling our electronic and traditional mailboxes.
- Corporations govern our time in myriad ways: by limiting the number of checkout clerks in a store and imposing long lines we have to stand in; by cutting customer service and placing the onus on the customer to use time-consuming automated telephone information lines; by having complicated and time-consuming return policies on purchases by mail; by eliminating free telephone airline purchases and forcing customers to spend hours searching websites for airline reservations. They do this not to sell us cheaper products but to maximize their profits.
- Corporations threaten our lives in many ways: by putting poisons into the environment, including our food and water supplies; by selling weapons without adequate control over who gets them and how they are used; by using packaging with health-damaging chemicals; by building housing developments in flood plains; by making dangerous products, even dangerous toys for children.

- Corporate-owned hospitals govern how women give birth. Because C-sections use fewer staff and save hospital time, hospitals make more money by scheduling C-sections instead of encouraging natural childbirth. To maximize their profits, they pressure families into a procedure that research shows has long-term negative psychological effects on mother and child.[21]
- Corporations threaten your home, as the mortgage crisis has made dramatically clear. Banks that hide the true cost of mortgages in the fine print are one kind of threat. Banks that package mortgages and sell them to speculators are another. Banks that borrow money at almost zero interest but don't pass the savings on to prospective homebuyers are a threat to prospective homebuyers with limited funds.
- Corporations control the government through lobbying and political contributions. Lobbyists for corporations often write our laws for corporate benefit, for their profit and our loss. Lobbying in such cases is a form of legalized corruption. And under *Citizens United,* corporations increasingly threaten our political process through the injection of unlimited corporate funding into elections.

We could go on. These are cases of corporate nuisance, intrusiveness, invasion, control, interference, oppression, theft, and even tyranny. When you add it all up, government by corporation is a major issue in American life, yet it is not included in public discourse.

There is a big difference between government by corporation and government by the representatives of the people. Corporations govern you for their profit and benefit, not yours. Governments govern citizens for the benefit of the citizenry as a whole. Governments govern openly. Citizens have imposed on their representatives a moral obligation to protect and empower everyone equally for the benefit of all. That's what democracy is. Governments have a right to govern because citizens, by voting, have given them that power. Governments are accountable to citizens; they have to make their actions transparent and justify them. And citizens can vote out their representatives if they feel that they are governing badly.

Corporations, however, govern your life for their own profit and benefit, not yours. They are transparent about it only if government requires them to be through regulation.

Government by corporation is a major *political* issue because conservatives have popularized the idea that government limits your liberty while the free market increases your liberty. But the opposite is true: for the most part, government works to protect your liberty from corporations that threaten to take it away in all the ways listed above and more. It is government regulation that limits the "liberty" of corporations to inflict harm. Corporations, when functioning properly, create enormous good on a daily basis in America, but they don't have to govern or threaten our lives to do so. For all of the above reasons, corporate governance of our lives needs to be part of public political discourse.

When you talk about the issue of government by corporations, keep in mind the details of what we outlined above. Extend the issue to examples that you may be specifically concerned with. Provide examples from your own life and the lives of citizens you represent or work for.

Here is what to say:
> ➤ *This debate is about **liberty** from **corporate government** and corporate meddling in our lives.*
> ➤ ***Corporations govern our lives** with almost no accountability. Due to a lack of regulations, corporations are in many cases **free and even encouraged to run our lives** in ways that are **intrusive, oppressive,** and even **tyrannical.***
> ➤ *Corporations **intrude on our personal lives,** collecting private information about us and snooping on the way we use our computers.*

➢ *We all have only **one precious life**, and our lifetime is a valuable good. Corporations **use our lifetime** to maximize their profits.*

➢ *Health insurance companies make decisions about **your health and your life**. Their decisions are governed by their own interest in maximizing profit. If health insurance companies are not regulated and if health care remains in private hands, you become **a bystander while others decide how healthy you will be and whether you will live**.*

➢ *On a daily basis, Americans face corporate **nuisance, intrusiveness, invasion, control, interference, oppression, theft,** and even **tyranny**. The massive control of corporations over our lives impinges on our most basic **freedoms**. To protect ourselves from this imposition, we need regulations.*

➢ *The **laissez-fair market limits your personal liberty**. Government—that is, people **who work for you** and are **accountable to you**—work to **protect your liberty**.*

➢ *Corporations govern you **for their profit and benefit, not yours**. They are **transparent** about it only if government requires them to be through regulation.*

➢ *The struggle over adequate regulations is between **corporations' interest** in making **maximal profit at your expense** and the government's interest in protecting your life and your liberty.*

➢ *Government regulations limit **corporations' ability to inflict harm on you in order to make a profit**.*

13

Predatory Privatization

Government in the American tradition has two major moral responsibilities: protection and empowerment. Protection goes well beyond the role of the military to include defense against crime, disease, natural disaster, environmental degradation, harm from unscrupulous companies, social injustice, the vicissitudes of childhood and old age, poverty, and food insecurity. Empowerment includes the public provision of resources on a large scale needed for commerce, human development, and civic improvement. Examples are public education, the system of roads and bridges, public buildings and institutions, water and sewer systems, agricultural assistance, financial institutions, energy provisions, and sponsored research. This is what we have called the Public. The Private, on the other hand, includes private property, business and industry, private financial institutions, private media, and religious institutions. What distinguishes the Private from the Public is that the Private entails no moral obligation to people in general.

Privatization is the transfer of public property, public functions, and public institutions into private hands. This includes the contracting out and outsourcing of public functions to private contractors.[22] Sometimes privatization is sensible, but it can sometimes be predatory. Privatization is predatory when, for the sake of profit, it removes or prevents protection and empowerment of the public at large or takes over other moral functions of government. A good example is the treatment of immigrants. One might think that trained government employees are in charge of detainment (actually imprisonment) and deportation of immigrants deemed undesirable. But as Thomas Gammel Toft-Hansen reports in the *New York Times,* these private contractors are actually fully in charge, without public control or oversight. There are no "outside supervisors, performance reports and monitoring mechanisms." This is a huge international private business. G4S, for example, is the largest of such private contractors, with 650,000 employees operating in countries all over the world.[23]

The line between sensible and predatory privatization is not always clear, but among the factors determining the difference are how a private company carries out the moral function of government and how much it charges the public.

When conservatives talk of "smaller government," what they really mean for the most part is the privatization of government, that is, the transfer of public property and functions into private hands. Conservatives have proposed the privatization of Medicare and Social Security, turning Medicare over to the private insurance industry and Social Security over to the stock market. Progressive resistance is based on moral grounds. Privatized Medicare would be subject to all the moral problems of private health insurance: high prices for the sake of profit, the restriction of authorizations with high administrative costs, and the lack of true universal coverage. Privatized Social Security would subject life savings to the vagaries of the market, putting retirement funds at risk and introducing the danger of funds running out for individuals who live long.

What is rarely, if ever, recognized is that privatization is already happening, in some cases irreversibly and on a grand scale. Much of it is sensible, with little or no moral downside, but a considerable amount of already existing privatization is predatory.

The Privatization of the Military

The armed forces and the Departments of Defense and State use private military companies such as Blackwater—whose name has been changed twice, to Xe and then to Academi—to train tens of thousands of security personnel to work in combat zones and other dangerous places around the world. The private military industry is worth over $100 billion a year. Private contractors make up 29 percent of the workforce in the U.S. intelligence community and cost the equivalent of 49 percent of their personnel budgets.[24] As the former secretary of defense Donald Rumsfeld pointed out, private military contractors are not subject to the Uniform Code of Military Justice.[25] They thus can do things that would be illegal for those in the U.S. military to do. Blackwater personnel alone have been accused of using excessive force on several occasions, including the killing of seventeen civilians in Iraq in 2007. In 2004 the CIA hired Blackwater contractors as part of a secret program to locate and assassinate top al Qaeda operatives, although it is unclear exactly what role Blackwater played.[26] Accusations abound, but little information has been released.

Military and intelligence operations are part of the moral mission of government, yet private contractors staff nearly a third of intelligence personnel positions and perform military duties without being subject to military law.[27]

The Privatization of Schools

Certain companies have set up widespread chains of corporate-owned charter schools, taking over public buildings and luring local students with claims of superior education while hiring teachers with little training at lower salaries and no or meager benefits and pensions. And all of this is paid for with government money that would otherwise go to support public schools. The public schools meanwhile lose their building spaces and funding for teacher salaries and pensions as money goes instead to profits for the charter school owners. Some charter school companies actively try to put public schools out of business. And some charter schools pay their principals hundreds of thousands of dollars a year but pay teachers a pittance. Moreover charter schools tend to teach to the test, turning schools into testing factories and undermining learning. Yet on the whole, charter schools do not perform better than public schools (though there are exceptions).[28] Control over our children's education has been handed over to private companies.

The Privatization of Water

All over America and in the third world, water is being privatized. Conservative antitax movements often result in cutting the funds necessary for maintaining clean water, water resources, sewage treatment, and water delivery systems. When this happens, corporations move in and offer to buy and maintain the groundwater and the whole water system. All too often the push for corporate profits means higher prices, less regulation, pollution and decrease in water quality, environmental damage, dumping of raw sewage, and lack of maintenance for water equipment. In some cases, corporations will even extract a community's groundwater, bottle it, and sell it back to the citizens at an inflated price. When water becomes a business, citizens become customers who are trapped into buying the company's water.

The Privatization of Regulation

The business of regulation itself has become privatized in a number of areas.

When it comes to regulating the quality of bottled drinking water, the government is at best marginally involved. FDA oversight doesn't apply to water that is packaged and sold in the same state. This leaves 60 to 70 percent of bottled water free of FDA regulation, and since most states do not have anywhere near adequate staff to regulate bottled water, the companies are left to regulate themselves.[29]

When government has inadequate resources to regulate financial affairs, financial regulation is outsourced to private accounting firms. The Enron scandal showed what can happen. Enron, with friends in high places in the government, applied for and received permission to get around regulation. As a result, executives faked economic accounts and embezzled enormous amounts of money from investors. Shareholders lost nearly $11 billion. Arthur Andersen, an accounting firm, colluded with Enron, earning $25 million dollars in audit fees and $27 million in consulting fees in just the year 2000.[30] And a significant cause of the 2008 economic crash was the failure by rating agencies to accurately rate the value of securities. Moody's, one of the most powerful rating agencies, gave AAA ratings to securities it knew were toxic, resulting in a huge loss to those who bought them. In other words, the de facto regulation of securities was in the hands of private companies whose job it is to maximize profit. Regulation, a public concern, had been privatized.

The explosion of the Deepwater Horizon oil rig not only killed eleven workers but also released a huge amount of oil into the Gulf of Mexico, killing large numbers of shorebirds, fish, and plant life, wiping out the fishing and shrimping industries along the Gulf for many years, and resulted in negative health effects on humans living there. A year later, dolphins and whales continued to die at twice the normal rate. The explosion itself resulted from the privatization of regulation. BP and its partners, Halliburton and Transocean, were effectively their own safety regulators, and as always they put profit ahead of safety. They did not install enough devices to stabilize the well; they did not wait for the results of tests on the foam used to seal the well; and they ignored the results of an important pressure test, among other mistakes. As a result, gases entered the well, rose, and exploded.

We could go on and on and on with examples, but our point is clear: privatization of a moral governmental function—protection of the public—is already with us and affecting us in ways we sometimes hardly realize.

Smaller Government and Predatory Privatization

When government carries out its protection and empowerment responsibilities, it does so for the public good, not for private profit, thus keeping those responsibilities within a moral realm. When those responsibilities are privatized and carried out for private profit, financial and other private interests overwhelm the public good, as seen in the instances discussed. This is precisely what conservatives have in mind when they argue for "smaller government."

Here is what to say:
➤ *Government has a **moral duty** to protect and empower its people. Private corporations have no such duty to citizens, which is why maintaining a **robust Public** is absolutely necessary to ensure everyone's well-being, prosperity, and safety.*
➤ *Privatization is the transfer of public property, public functions, and public institutions into private hands. Often privatization works well. But where **people's basic protection and empowerment** are concerned, it is **the government's duty** to preserve the freedom of citizens.*
➤ *Privatization can be **predatory** and downright immoral when, for the sake of profit, it **removes or prevents the protection and empowerment of the public,** whether by handing our kids' edu-*

81

cation over to corporations or putting our water supply in corporate hands.

➤ *Privatization makes the life of citizens **more expensive**: corporations work to **maximize profit** with no moral obligation to customers. They offer services and goods **at the price the market will bear**. Basic protections and empowerments often cost more when they are put in the hands of corporations rather than left in the hands of the public, **which is not concerned with making a profit**.*

➤ *Conservatives arguing for "smaller government" know full well that protection and empowerment functions—education, military protection, and clean drinking water—are needed by the American people. "Smaller government" **means making the public good secondary** and abandoning the sacred moral missions of the government.*

14

Workers Are Profit Creators

Corporations can profit only if people work for them. Workers are therefore profit creators for the corporations, their stockholders, and their top management.

Corporations, however, divide the people who work for them into two classes: assets and resources. The assets are the top management, the financial experts, and the technical experts. They are the most valued people, hired by headhunting agencies, given stock options, respected, treated well, and paid well with salaries. All the other workers are seen as resources, on par with material resources like steel and fuel, to be used efficiently and exploited maximally at minimal cost. They are central to profit creation, yet they get little or no respect, are interchangeable, and are paid as little as possible with wages. Individually they are powerless, and so they perform best, and cost the corporation the most, when represented by a union. Asset employees tend not to be represented by unions since they are inherently valued.

Health care coverage and pensions make up part of the pay earned by workers. Pensions are deferred payments for work done over a long period. Why do corporations provide benefits like health care insurance and pensions? Partly because unions demand them, but also because they help a company stay profitable. Corporations like to have workers who are loyal and know the company, which helps companies avoid the costs of recruiting and training new employees or operating with untrained employees. Health care coverage and pensions buy loyalty and so add to profits by minimizing the costs of recruitment and training.

Much of this is not part of ordinary public discourse. Workers are neither thought of nor talked about as profit creators. The profit-making aspects of health care benefits and pensions, and the fact that they are deferred payments for work done, are rarely part of public political and economic discourse. Nor are the ethical responsibilities that commitments to these deferred payments place on corporations. Corporations have an ethical responsibility to pay *in full* for work done. That means they have an ethical responsibility to set aside funds to pay for health care coverage and pensions that are part of the pay for work done. Yet corporations often spend such funds on other items, including capital investment, stockholder dividends, and payments and bonuses to top managers. To avoid paying for work already performed, they may lay off loyal employees and hire younger ones for less money or outsource work to companies with no such obligations to their workers. This provides more profit for the corporation, but it amounts to *theft* from the employees—theft of earned payment for previously done work.

This description is, of course, written from a progressive perspective, one of empathy for workers and support for their cause on the moral basis of progressive fairness and reciprocity. The conservative view is very different; from a laissez-faire free market perspective, workers *individually* sell their labor to the company for a price: their wages. Unions are seen as unfairly inflating the price of labor, and do so immorally since they violate the principle of individual responsibility and force workers to pay for the union's services. In "right to work" states, union shops are banned, and unions become weak or nonexistent since workers do not have to pay union dues and companies do not have to hire union workers. This is a conservative ideal since it fits the principle of individual rather than social responsibility and is seen as fair because what is fair is what you contract for. Health care benefits and pensions are seen by conservatives as "extras," add-ons to wages rather than part of payment for work done. And since these extras are mainly negotiated by unions, they are seen as illegitimate uses of collectivism, which violates purely individual responsibility. Conservatives see unions as a form of socialism, anathema to individual responsibility and the rights of corporations to maximize profits. As to the class difference between asset employees and resource employees, that is acceptable since asset employees are seen as meriting their higher status by adding value to the company.

Right now the conservative perspective dominates public discourse. The progressive perspective is largely undiscussed and needs to be introduced and repeated over and over.

Here is what to say:
- ➤ *Workers are **profit creators**. Corporations can profit only if people work for them.*
- ➤ *Health care benefits and pensions are part of the **pay earned by** workers. They are **deferred payments for work done**.*
- ➤ *Health care benefits and pensions **benefit the workers** and **the companies that provide them**.*
- ➤ *Health care benefits and pensions **add to profits**. They buy loyalty so that companies can **avoid** the **costs of recruiting and training new employees** as well as the **costs of operating with untrained employees**.*
- ➤ *Corporations have an ethical responsibility to **pay in full for** work done. **That includes benefits and pensions**.*
- ➤ *Companies are **ethically responsible** for setting aside funds for workers' deferred payments and **not using them for anything else**. **Spending** those funds—on capital investment, stockholder dividends, or payments and bonuses to top managers—is **unethical**.*

15

Public Education Benefits All and Protects Freedom

The Founding Fathers were right: public education is necessary for a democracy as well as a vibrant economy. Freedom requires education. You are not free if you don't know what's possible for you, what affects you, and how to do things you care about. Education is centrally about self-realization, about what you are free to become.

You are not free if you are not an educated citizen who can play his or her part in a democracy. Educated citizens have to know about the full range of issues that concern their society, and they have to be able to understand the background of these issues.

No society can maintain liberty without freethinking people and access to knowledge. Imagine if access to information of any kind cost what a first-class education can cost, upward of forty thousand dollars a year. Only the wealthiest could afford it, and since knowledge is power, money would run society without challenge.

We are now moving in that direction.

We all benefit from an educated public. We want the doctor we see to be well educated by a system of medical training that is open and where all findings are available to all doctors. The same is true of engineers and architects. We need our buildings and bridges to stand up and our cars to work. This requires a wide system of education and knowledge available to the public.

We all benefit from a widespread educational system because no one of us can have all the knowledge we need to get through life. We need others who know what we don't. The more education is limited to an elite, the more it will cost to access that knowledge. Highly specialized and skilled experts, from corporate lawyers to neurosurgeons, command high fees. The more critical knowledge is monopolized by privatized higher education, the more expensive it becomes.

A democratic society requires education that is both widespread and deep. It is a social matter. Every day we depend on others being educated, both for the practical things in life and for our political freedom.

The conservative view of education can be thought of as the application of the laissez-faire free market. Good grades are profits; bad grades are losses. Greed is good. Classmates are competitors, not cooperators. Grade inflation is a metaphorical version of economic inflation. The more good grades there are, the less valuable they are. Innate talent that makes school easy is like being born wealthy, but for most students it is assumed that success is a direct consequence of discipline. The lack of natural talent is like being born poor; the only way to succeed is through discipline, by pulling yourself up by your bootstraps.

Given this understanding of education, it is natural to view even public education as a business. Schools whose students get good test scores are profitable. Teachers of those good students bring in profit and, like executives who earn bonuses, deserve merit pay. Schools whose students regularly get bad test scores are unprofitable and considered failing schools. Like divisions of companies that lose money, they can be closed down, and just as managers whose divisions regularly lose money stand to get fired, so do teachers whose students don't get high test scores.

Several things are missed in this analogy. There are many students who live in poverty and dire circumstances, which can lead them to gang membership, crime, and drugs. Many of our best teachers volunteer to teach in schools with such students in the hope of saving them from such fates, whether or not they get good grades. Such teachers deserve respect and merit pay, not firing. In addition, teaching to the test is not real teaching. Students with good test scores may not be well-educated people, much less become better citizens or community members or parents. Good test-takers may not add to our store of knowledge, may not care about sharing their knowledge or contributing to our freedom.

When education is seen as a business, privatization of public education seems like a natural alternative. Though there are some locally run charter schools that do somewhat better than public schools, they are exceptions. On the whole, charter schools perform no better than public schools, and they place the moral responsibility of education in the hands of profit-seeking corporations.

Here is what to say:

➤ *Public education is necessary for a democracy and a vibrant economy. You can be free only if you live in a free society, and no society can be free without freethinking people and freedom of access to knowledge.*

➤ *Democratic freedom requires education. You are not free if you don't know what is possible for you, what affects you, and how to do things you care about.*

➤ *We all benefit from our educational system, whether or not we as individuals happen to have the knowledge we need. Indeed no one of us can have all the knowledge we need to get through life. We need others to be knowledgeable. Whether or not we happen to be in school, we are using the educational system.*

➤ *The more education is limited to an elite, the more it will cost to access the knowledge education offers. Highly specialized and skilled experts command high fees. The more critical knowl-*

edge is monopolized by privatized higher education, the more expensive it becomes.

➤ *A democratic society requires education that is both widespread and deep. Every day we depend on others being educated, both for practical things and for our political freedom. In a democracy, knowledge needs to be democratized, and the democratization of knowledge can come only through public education.*

16

Rethinking Food

The discovery was startling. We are not separate from nature, from the physical world and from each other. The integration of the body with the physical world is hardwired in the brain.

At the University of Parma in the 1990s, systems of mirror neurons and canonical neurons were discovered.[31] Mirror neurons in the brain fire both when you perform an action and when you see someone else perform the same action. Through connections to the emotional regions in the brain, mirror neuron systems allow us to tell how others feel. This is the basis of empathy toward other humans and animals. Canonical neuron systems fire when you see an object or perform a canonical action on that object. A canonical action is what you typically do with an object: peel a banana, bite into an apple, crack open a coconut, and so on, as opposed to stepping on a banana or balancing an apple on your nose.

Mirror and canonical neuron systems directly integrate us with the physical world, whether with other beings or with physical objects. Nature is not outside of us. It is in us. We take air into our lungs, water courses through our bodies, we ingest plants and animal parts that in turn become part of our body. The meat we eat, the wine or soda we drink, the outdoor grill smoke we inhale, and the fumes from cars and electric power plants all come to rest in our bodies. The term *environment* is therefore misleading. Environmentalism is centrally about *you* and what enters and becomes part of your body, as well as the way your body is part of nature.

Nature is most obviously in us in the case of food. We get most of our food from corporate agriculture, and corporate agriculture is chin-deep in politics. The place where food and politics come together is the Farm Bill, a comprehensive piece of legislation passed by Congress every five to seven years. It is really a food bill. It is about what we pay as a nation to produce food and what kind of food we get for it. The original idea was that the government should pay to make sure the nation's farmers produce enough food for our people. Yet while sufficient food has not been a real issue for some time, we still pay out a huge amount of money. The questions to ask are *What do we get for what we pay?* and *Who do the payments go to?*

The news is mixed. Some is good, but a lot of it is bad and in need of change. Let's start with the payments.

If you think the payments are going mostly to families working on farms, you may be surprised. In 2010 some 90,000 checks, amounting to $394 million dollars, went out to wealthy investors and absentee landowners[32]—people who do not actually work the land. And huge amounts of money go to large, corporate-owned producers who take a hefty profit off the top of generous subsidies.

For example, what is called "crop insurance" in the Farm Bill is actually *profit insurance,* essentially a transfer of funds from taxpayers to mostly corporate growers. The government pays 60 percent of the insurance cost. The base of the insurance is the most profitable recent year. If crop income falls below 95 percent of the most profitable year, the insurance makes up the difference. That is, growers are guaranteed at the least 95 percent of their most profitable year, with the government paying more than half of the insurance cost. In addition, the insurance companies—there are sixteen of them—are mostly owned by corporations from abroad. Our government guarantees those companies a profit of 14 percent a year. Two-thirds of the subsidized growers grow cotton, corn, rice, wheat, and soybeans. That's right: cotton. How much cotton have you eaten recently? How much corn-based ethanol?

By way of contrast, from 1995 to 2010 apple farms received $261 million in subsidies, while cotton received more than $31 billion.[33] We are giving money to the largest growers of some of the most profitable crops, and many of these crops are not used for food at all.

So what should we expect from the Farm Bill? At least two things: healthy food and food aid for those who can't afford food otherwise.

On the food aid side, the food bill has done well, but it is under attack by conservatives. The technical name for food aid is the Supplemental Nutrition Assistance Program (SNAP), which really amounts to food stamps and is a stellar example of Americans taking care of each other. The part of the Farm Bill that went to the food aid program was about two-thirds of the $96.3 billion spent in 2010.

A full 14.5 percent of Americans are victims of "food insecurity,"[34] jargon for not knowing where your next meal is coming from. Those food stamps are necessary, yet they are a prime target of conservatives looking to cut "spending," looking to eliminate what our fellow Americans desperately need. More than 40 percent of food stamps go to children and 20 percent to the disabled. It works.

But after food stamps are paid for, the Farm Bill still pays out $32 billion per year. How much of that gets us healthy food? Not much. Healthy food is food that is nutritious and not harmful. On a balanced food plate, fruits, vegetables, legumes, and nuts constitute about half. How much do these healthy foods get of the Department of Agriculture subsidies? Two percent.[35]

What is harmful food? There are two basic kinds: food containing poisons and food that leads to disease. Roughly 68 percent of Americans adults and 20 percent of children are obese or overweight.[36] Obesity leads to diabetes, heart disease, high blood pressure, stroke, and a high risk of certain cancers. The health care system spends considerable money to treat nutrition-based chronic diseases: $147 billion on obesity, $116 billion on diabetes, and hundreds of billions more to treat cardiovascular disease and the cancers that have been linked to harmful food. Obesity itself accounts for nearly a tenth of all spending on health care.[37] In most cases, obesity is due to poor diet. The main food culprits are well known: sugar and high-fructose corn syrup, fats, starches, and processed foods in general.

The Farm Bill has a lot to answer for here. These foods—harmful foods—are highly subsidized and so cost less to consumers and bring more profit to corporate producers. The Farm Bill pays enormous subsidies to agribusiness to produce these harmful foods and does nothing to discourage or ban them. Those in Congress and those in the Department of Agriculture who either promote these subsidies or do nothing to stop the production of cheap harmful food are neglecting their obligations to their fellow citizens. They are using money from citizens to harm citizens in the name of corporate profit.

What about poisons in food? The obvious cases are pesticides, herbicides, and toxic fertilizers made from toxic heavy metals, toxic chemicals, and sometimes even radioactive waste.[38] These fertilizers are used nationwide, and there is no federal law requiring that they be listed as ingredients in the foods we eat. The Department of Agriculture does not use Farm Bill money to monitor and stop the practice. There are, of course, other farm safety issues: e coli and other harmful bacteria and viruses regularly contaminate our food supply. Yet the total Farm Bill expenditure on food safety is only 0.9 percent of the budget.[39] Less than 1 percent is spent to monitor and prevent direct corporate poisoning of our food supply.

But aside from these rather obvious poisons, there are other, more hidden poisons in food. Meat and fish are commonly laced with growth hormones and antibiotics. They are fed to fish and animals, and we who eat those fish and animals take them into our bodies. Why are they in the fish and meat in the first place? Because of agricultural practices not only sanctioned but actually subsidized under the Farm Bill. Cattle are corralled on huge, tightly crowded feedlots by the tens of thousands. Their dung not only pollutes the soil; it breeds disease that spreads from steer to steer. To try to stop the spread of disease on the feedlots the cattle are injected with antibiotics. The same is true of factory chickens, pigs, and fish that are packed in tightly crowded conditions, where their massive amounts of dung also spread disease, and so they have to be injected with or fed antibiotics as well.

Why are fish and animals raised this way? For corporate profit. It saves money to raise fish and animals in factory conditions.

Aside from the nontrivial moral issue of animal cruelty in these cases, the fact is we are being fed those antibiotics when we eat the meat of these animals. Besides the possibility that the disease has not been completely prevented, the antibiotics themselves compromise our health and immune systems. The overuse of antibiotics leads to the development of resistant strains of bacteria and viruses. And antibiotics compromise our immune systems. It is like being on a constant dose of antibiotics, which kills friendly bacteria in your body that are necessary for health and leaves you vulnerable to antibiotic-resistant viruses and bacteria. Since it is hard to develop new antibiotics, their overuse in corporate agriculture can harm us and leave us unresponsive to medical treatment when we need it. This is not a direct form of poisoning, but it can have the same effect. Foods derived from genetically modified organisms (GMOs), which are so widespread that it is hard to avoid them, fall into a similar class of indirect poisoning. Their genes have been modified so that they produce poisons to kill bugs and weeds. We eat those bug and weed poisons when we consume GMO foods.

What about organic food, which has none of the poisons and

is almost entirely healthy? A tiny amount, about 0.1 percent, was allocated in the most recent Farm Bill for organic research and a program to help organic farmers.

The moral is clear. The Farm Bill provides public money to private, mostly corporate agriculture. It should be an example of a robust Public promoting protection and empowerment for all our citizens, promoting and subsidizing healthy food and discouraging, monitoring, and when necessary banning harmful and poisonous food.

The Farm Bill should become the Healthy Food Bill.

Here is what to say:

➤ *The Farm Bill should promote and subsidize* **healthy food** *and discourage, ban, or at least not subsidize* **harmful food.**

➤ *We shouldn't give* **public money** *to mostly corporate agriculture that puts profit ahead of safe and healthy food.*

➤ **Sun food** *is food grown organically and locally.* **Oil food** *is grown with petroleum-based pesticides and insecticides or uses a lot of oil to be shipped long distances. Most funding goes to* **oil food** *and almost nothing to* **sun food.** *That should be reversed.*

➤ *Farm Bill funds should* **feed people.** **Food stamps prevent hunger, if not starvation.**

➤ *Poisons should be removed from food. That includes* **pesticides, herbicides, antibiotics,** *and* **toxic fertilizers,** *especially those with* **radioactive waste.**

➤ *Crop insurance is profit insurance. Taxpayers shouldn't be wasting* **food money** *on it.*

17

Systemic Effects in Nature
and Economics

Nature is systemic. Causes in nature arise less by direct action than by systemic causation, but the systemic aspect of nature is hard to see and express. Every language has a way of expressing direct causation in its grammar.[40] No language has a way of expressing systemic causation in its grammar. Systemic structure is just hard to understand and discuss.

Before we go into the details of systemic causation, we should point out its political role. It is a natural idea for liberals. If you ask liberals about the causes of crime, you will get a systemic account: endemic poverty, lack of education, bad neighborhoods, or neglectful parenting due to economic hardships. If you ask conservatives, you will get a direct causation account: criminals are bad people.

The difference is due to different moral frames. In the strict father moral frame, morality is a matter of following simple moral rules, of doing what you are told, which takes discipline and direct action. Failure to obey the rules requires punishment, which leads directly to self-discipline. In short, strict father morality is structured by the idea of direct causation. Thus conservatives object to, for instance, explanations of global warming because they involve systems.

The following are some of the properties of ecological systems, which cannot be treated as cases of direct causation.

- *Homeostasis:* Just as a rubber band stretches a bit and returns to form, so natural systems under normal conditions stay within certain bounds and are self-correcting.
- *Feedback:* Some changes produce more of the same change and build on themselves. That is positive feedback. Other changes produce less of the same change and tend to undo themselves. That is negative feedback. An example of positive feedback is the melting polar ice cap. The ice cap reflects light and heat. As the Earth warms, the ice cap melts. The more it melts, the less heat it reflects and the more heat is absorbed into the atmosphere. So the Earth gets progressively hotter, which tends to melt the ice cap more. And the cycle continues.
- *Nonlocal causation:* Nonlocal causation is causation at a distance, often in a chain of more direct causes. For example, as the Earth heats, the water in the oceans heat up and more water evaporates, say, in the Pacific Ocean. That atmospheric water is then blown by west-to-east winds over Canada and the North Pole, and in winter on the East Coast it falls as snow. Thus heat in the Pacific can produce snow on the East Coast.
- *Nonlinear causation:* A small change can produce a large change. For example, the decision by oil-drilling managers to use slightly cheaper materials was a relatively small change, but it resulted in the huge BP oil spill in the Gulf of Mexico.
- *Cross-category causation:* A change intended in one conceptual domain may have effects in other domains. For example, the Yangtze River dam in China, intended only to provide hydroelectric power, will displace tens of thousands of villagers and likely change the rotation of the Earth.
- *Probabilistic effects:* Effects within a certain range will definitely occur, but one cannot predict exactly when and where, exactly how great, and in what form. For example, the amount of heat

in the Gulf of Mexico increases the energy in hurricanes produced over the Gulf. This results in more, and more powerful,
hurricanes. But you can't predict any particular hurricane. So
if you ask, *Did global warming cause Hurricane Katrina?*, you
are asking the wrong question, since particular hurricanes are
probabilistic. But if you ask, *Was the likelihood and ferocity of
Hurricane Katrina caused by global warming?*, the answer is yes
because the accumulated heat produced the increased energy
that in turn produced the greater ferocity and likelihood of
storms on the Gulf.

Direct causation, by contrast, has different properties. Effects
occur at the same time, in the same place, and at the same scale as
the cause. The effects don't undo themselves, nor do they build on
themselves. Nature does not work this way; it can be understood
only systemically. A good example is the Keystone XL pipeline.
The conservative argument is that it will create jobs. Actually it
will create only about 2,500 to 4,650 short-term jobs building the
pipeline.[41] But more important it will have enormous systemic
effects. The Canadian tar sands oil pits lie under an enormous
boreal forest, which sequesters a huge amount of carbon dioxide and is the only habitat for some of the largest populations of
woodland caribou left in the world; in addition, 30 percent of
North America's songbirds and 40 percent of its waterfowl rely
on the wetlands and waterways of the boreal forest. Getting at the
tar sands requires clear-cutting thousands of acres of the boreal
forests, diverting rivers, and strip-mining. Destroying that forest will certainly make those species of songbirds go extinct, and
the carbon dioxide held by the boreal forest will be released, significantly increasing global warming. Moreover tar sands oil is
dirty and sticky; it's tar, after all. To get it to flow it must have
heat, which is supplied by a huge amount of natural gas pumped
to the tar pits. Why not use the natural gas itself for fuel instead
of the tar? Because the price of gas is a lot lower than the price

of oil, meaning there is more profit for oil companies to be made from oil.

The destruction of the forest and the species as well as the increase in global warming do not enter the cost equation for oil companies because they are *negative systemic effects*. Negative systemic effects are real effects that are not counted in direct causation computations. They happen outside of a given frame and so are not taken into account when that frame, and only that frame, is used. In this case, the frame is that of oil company profit.

But there are additional negative systemic effects. Heat is not enough to get tar to flow. To get the tar out of the ground, you have to pump in a huge amount of water and toxic chemicals. The water sinks underneath the sticky oil, pushing it up, and the toxic chemicals help to break down the stickiness of the tar. The water used is so polluted by the toxic chemicals that it is rendered unfit to drink. The oil companies do not pay for the water; they simply drain the aquifer it comes from while letting much of the poisoned water stay in the ground.

In order to get the poisoned water and tar mixture to flow, it must be heated to 150 degrees Fahrenheit and then put into the pipeline. The pipe is huge, three feet in diameter, enough to carry up to 900,000 *barrels* per day. The steel the pipe is made of is 0.465 inches thick, less than half an inch. Along the 1,700 miles of the pipeline the steel is exposed to 1,600 pounds of force per square inch. This is twice as much force as there was in the Exxon-Mobil pipeline that exploded and spilled 42,000 gallons of oil into the Yellowstone River.

The steel for the pipe is made in China and India. Just one flaw in the steel along the 1,700 miles, or one mistake by a worker doing the pipefitting, and you will have a huge explosion releasing a vast amount of hot poisoned water plus tar, which will sink into the local water table and aquifer and cannot be cleaned up. The surrounding land will become uninhabitable.

What is the likelihood of a spill? The existing Keystone I tar sands pipeline has spilled more than twelve times in its first twelve months of operation. How serious were these spills? In July 2010 a spill of more than 800,000 gallons of toxic tar sands crude from the Enbridge pipeline contaminated more than thirty miles of water and shoreline along the Kalamazoo River in Michigan. This created public health problems, threats to groundwater, widespread fish kills, and destruction of wildlife habitat, contamination that is still being cleaned up at a cost exceeding $700 million.[42] Government tests indicated that defective steel may have been used in up to ten sections of the pipe. Keystone XL will use steel from the same Indian manufacturer.

The real-time leak detection system does not register spills less than 700,000 gallons per day (1.5 to 2 percent of its capacity).[43] In other words, the company, TransCanada, doesn't worry about, or even notice, a "little" spill under 700,000 gallons per day. The spill detection system is calibrated not to massive contamination of drinking water, land, and habitat, but only to the cost of lost crude.

Refining the poisoned water plus tar into crude oil is expensive, and the final product is very low quality oil. It will not help offset the price of a gallon of gas because oil, including this oil, goes on the world market, where the needs of developing countries like China drive up the price. No amount of excess oil coming from the United States will significantly drop the price of oil, since the United States produces only 10 percent of the world market at present. In fact the pipeline will increase oil prices in the U.S. Midwest, as TransCanada acknowledged. It estimates an increase in cost to the United States for Canadian crude between $2 billion and $3.9 billion per year.[44]

What will be gained from Keystone XL? Short-term profits for oil companies. The only thing that permits those profits is that major costs are not paid by the companies involved but by U.S. citizens: the "free" water used in the aquifers, the "free" cost of the arboreal forests, the "free" costs of songbird extinction, the "free" cost of risk—major risk, and largely uninsured and uninsurable risk. The risks are borne by millions of people living along the pipeline, now and for decades to come.

As we hope this discussion shows, the Keystone XL pipeline is more than just a long pipe: it is a project embedded in ecological and economic systems of enormous complexity. Systemic causation matters, but it is not in the public discourse. What we find instead are casual declarations of politicians. Here is Mitt Romney, the Republican Party's nominee for president: "Of course we should build the Keystone Pipeline. We should drill in the Gulf, North Dakota, drill in Alaska and take advantage of our energy resources."[45] For Romney, a business executive whose expertise lies in what makes the most profit for corporations, those systemic complexities don't matter. What matters is profit. "We once built an Interstate Highway System and the Hoover Dam. Now we can't even build a pipeline. . . . We once led the world in manufacturing and exports, investment. Today, we lead the world in lawsuits. You know, when we replace a law professor with *a conservative businessman as president,* that's going to end."[46]

The neglect of systemic costs is not a matter of ignorance or not paying attention. Corporations carefully plan for what, in economic jargon, is called "the externalization of cost and risk," that is, placing the costs and risks on the public. This is done every day, everywhere—wherever a company dumps its pollutants or waste into the air or a river or leaves a toxic pool from fracking on a farmer's land. It is part of the business model: making a profit by not paying the full cost of doing business, and placing that cost on the public or on isolated individuals who are helpless to resist the forces of large corporations.

It is dumping, planned dumping, but worse than dumping in itself. Surreptitiously transferring costs and risks to the public is the economic and moral equivalent of theft. The reason is that money is fungible: giving a debit is equivalent to taking a credit.

But the costs and risks are not just financial. They include health costs and life risks placed on ordinary people without their knowledge or consent—just for profit. This is immoral.

Keystone XL is thus a paradigm case of systemic causation, but conservatives miss the systemic and think only in terms of direct causation, which fits well with the emphasis on individual responsibility. This is why conservatives are more willing to help blameless victims of natural disaster than help homeless people, who conservatives perceive as being directly responsible for their own circumstances. When liberals argue systemic causation, conservatives see that as making excuses for individual shortcomings.

Here is what to say:

> ➤ *Dirty energy industries—oil, coal, and natural gas—make a lot of their money by **not cleaning up**. They profit by not paying the full costs of doing business and instead **placing those costs on the public**.*
> ➤ *Nature is never free. Taking or destroying it places costs elsewhere.*
> ➤ *When corporations take "free" water for fracking, "free" boreal forests for tar oil, and our "free" air and water to dump their pollution, we bear the cost.*
> ➤ *Surreptitiously transferring costs and risks to the public is the economic and moral equivalent of theft.*

18

An Infrastructure
for Eternal Energy

Given the overwhelming scientific evidence for man-made global warming, it might seem surprising that there are still people, almost all conservatives, denying its existence. Actually, it is not surprising at all.

In the strict father family, there is no authority higher than the father. This moral system is projected onto the conservative view of the market. As seen in the conservative slogan "Let the market decide," the market itself is the decider, with no authority above it. The market is seen as natural (assuming greed is a natural human trait) and moral (if all follow their self-interest, the interests of all will be maximized). Thus in extreme conservatism there should be nothing and no one above the market. That means no government regulation, no taxation, no labor rights or worker rights, and no tort cases. And though science can serve the market—as in nuclear power, deep-water drilling, and labor-saving technology—science that contradicts the market is interference.

Science tells us that considerations of global warming require phasing out the old polluting energies—coal, gas, and oil—as soon as possible and replacing them with energy sources that are eternally present, clean, and free: solar, wind, water, and soil energies. With the right subsidies these eternal energy sources would soon become competitive. But the polluting energy companies have made discoveries of vast gas and oil reserves in the United States and they want to profit from them. Their current profits are significantly increased by generous subsidies from ordinary taxpayers. They want their subsidies to continue, and they do not want subsidies given to a competing clean, eternal, free energy industry. Nor do they want environmental reviews that might kill proposed projects and get in the way of profits. Here corporate interests merge with conservative ideology, which rules out serious regulation of the energy market.

Science is the most dangerous area for conservatism. Science seeks the truth, and the truth does not always support conservative ideals and myths. When it doesn't, as in the case of global warming and evolution, it must be challenged.

Thus even in the face of overwhelming converging scientific evidence some conservatives argue that global warming is "just a theory." Some conservatives will use an error in one study or by a single scientist to discount the entirety of the scientific consensus on the issue. Some conservatives claim that scientists are political liberals engaged in a plot. The techniques are the same used against Galileo; only the targets are relatively recent.

The conservatives are losing, but their media blitz has been hiding the fact. Currently 83 percent of Americans acknowledge the fact that global warming is happening, and 72 percent believe that human behavior is substantially responsible for it; 71 percent trust scientists; 75 percent want the government to institute regulations to stop global warming; and over 40 percent believe that global warming is a very or extremely important political issue.[47]

It is thus crucial for progressives to point out the results of polluting energy sources: tar from Canada, black sludge in the Gulf of Mexico, black lungs from coal, and toxic dangers to water supplies from fracking. Polluting energy sources are dangerous, both in the long term and the short term. Nuclear waste is actually deadly radioactive material and will remain deadly for over ten thousand years, far longer than all of human history so far. There is no safe place to store it and no way to guard it for ten thousand years, and transporting it opens it to the possibility of terrorist attacks and other risks.

By contrast, energy from the sun, wind, water, and soil (biomass) is eternal, free, and clean. What is lacking right now is a robust eternal energy infrastructure with generators that convert the source (e.g., sunlight) to electricity and connectors that link generators to the grid. That infrastructure is becoming cheaper all the time, but its development needs subsidies, which are now going to dirty energy.

Energy Reality

Is all energy equal? The very use of the word *energy* for both dirty and clean sources suggests it is. Physicists even measure it in the same units. Yet the equivalence of energy types is a framing phenomenon, not an objective reality.

Just as a penny saved is a penny earned, so an erg saved is an erg earned. Energy is fungible. The more we save, the less we need to use. The more we use, the less we save. Conservation is every bit as important as production. That is why high gas mileage matters in cars and why insulation matters for buildings.

The fungibility frame, however important, is rarely used. It should be. But fungibility by itself hides another framed truth: saving is better, because not using dirty energy slows down global warming. Both frames, fungibility and saving is better, are important. They point toward a need to subsidize both generation and grid connection to guarantee the development of eternal, free, and clean energy sources, as well as subsidizing conservation efforts.

In contrast, the dirty energy companies are advertising a frame that hides these two truths. The energy freedom frame stresses energy independence and the need for more and more energy for the indefinite future. The ads promote oil drilling, gas fracking, and coal mining (without mentioning the removal of mountaintops). They are selling dirty energy as natural and clean—"natural" gas and "clean" coal—and as necessary for our economy. What is not mentioned is the fungibility of conservation, that energy waste is massive and that conservation efforts cut energy needs.

The dirty energy companies also use an equivalent energy frame, in which forms of energy are interchangeable and have a common measure. The companies are investing in many forms of one thing: energy. Coal is as good as solar; oil is a good as wind; natural gas is better than most. What the equivalent energy frame and the freedom frame hide is obvious: dirty fuels are dirty and clean fuels are clean.

Here is what to say:
- ➤ *It is time to phase out the **old polluting energies**—coal, gas, and oil—as soon as possible and replace them with energy sources that are **eternally present, clean, and free**: the **sun, wind, water, and soil** energies.*
- ➤ *We need to **clean up our energy**.*
- ➤ ***Phase out dirty energy. Don't prolong it with subsidies.***
- ➤ *Sun, wind, water, and soil are eternal energy sources.*
- ➤ *Eternal energy is the future. It's here now; it's free; it's clean.*
- ➤ *Nuclear power is a nuclear threat. Look at Japan.*
- ➤ *So-called **nuclear waste** is **highly radioactive** and will stay that way for over ten thousand years. It can **leak** or **be stolen and kill**. There is nothing clean about it. **Radiation pollution is the worst form of pollution**.*
- ➤ *Energy is fungible. The more we save, the less we need to use. The more we use, the less we save. **Just as a penny saved is a penny earned, so energy saved is energy produced. Conservation does as much for us as production. Save, don't drill.***

➤ *Good soil feeds us forever. In the long run, a farm's soil is worth more than the oil underneath. Don't drill.*

➤ *In terms of energy alone, conservation is equivalent to drilling. But drilling destroys, while conserving saves. Conservation, not drilling, should be subsidized.*

➤ *For citizens, conservation wins. For oil companies, drilling wins. Which matters more to you?*

➤ *Preventing conservation is wasting energy.*

★ ★ ★ ★

PART IV

A Phrasebook
for Democrats

We have several goals in this phrasebook. First is to warn against using language that is defined in terms of conservative values. Unfortunately Democrats have all too often used such language, thus shooting themselves in the foot by inadvertently promoting conservative morality and values. Second is to propose Democratic language where it is lacking. Third, and most important, is to explain *why* we are making these suggestions.

19

The Economy and the Public

Let's walk directly into the minefield. Over the past thirty years, conservatives have made *taxes* a dirty word. *Tax* has come to mean hard-earned money that the government takes out of your pocket and wastes on undeserving people and projects. *Taxes* used to be a positive term meaning money paid for worthwhile and valuable government projects that make people's lives better. Indeed such projects used to bear the sign "Your Taxes at Work." The positive sense is still there in the word *taxpayer,* which refers to an upright, responsible citizen who pays his or her taxes readily and expects the money to be used for worthwhile projects and programs.

But for the most part, conservatives have brought the negative meaning into political discourse, often with the help of Democrats. Take the phrase *tax relief.* In the frame defining *relief* there is an affliction, an afflicted party, and a reliever who relieves the affliction. The reliever is a hero, and those who create the affliction or don't want it relieved are villains. When *tax* is added to *relief,* we get the metaphor "Taxation is an affliction," with the implication that anyone against tax relief is a villain. This metaphor makes sense only in a conservative moral system, and so the use of the words evokes not only the relief frame and the metaphor, but also the moral system needed to make sense of it.

The phrase "Taxation is an affliction" was introduced by George

W. Bush on his first day in office and became a conservative mantra in public discourse. Since then Democrats have adopted it in such phrases as *middle-class tax relief* and *tax relief for small businesses*. This helps conservatives by getting their moral system into the brains of voters.

Tax burden is a similar case. Burdens weigh you down, making it hard to get anywhere or do the things you want to do. When you add *tax*, you get the metaphor "Taxes are burdens," limiting how you can move or act. Those who call for lower taxes are heroes who are taking the burden off your shoulders.

Tax havens and *tax loopholes* also define taxes as evils to escape from. A haven is a pleasant place, safe from harm. Here taxes are can harm you if you don't get away from them. *Tax paradise* works similarly. A loophole is a hole you can escape through so as not to be caught in the net of taxes. *Avoiding taxes* and *evading taxes* portray taxes as evils that can catch and harm you. Even though tax evasion is a crime, the metaphor of evading taxes portrays taxes as the evil. The term *tax cuts* works similarly. It implies that taxes are too high and that **lowering them** is always good.

A sneaky example of conservative tax framing is the *death tax*, a name for the Inheritance Tax, which applies only to people who inherit more than $5 million. Their inheritance is taxed just as if it were earned income. However, the term *death tax* suggests that it is a tax applying to everyone since everyone dies. This is an intentionally deceitful expression, while the other frames are simply expressions of the conservative moral system applied to economics.

One way to avoid using such conservative language is to speak of **revenue** instead of taxes whenever possible. **Revenue** is a word from business and refers to income needed to operate an institution, which is what tax revenue is for. **Revenue** focuses on the use of the money, not on who's paying it or who gets it. It avoids the negative connotations.

In the context of money used for the Public, **revenue** is a fairly neutral word that allows for certain truths to be told. One can speak of **revenue depletion** and **revenue neglect** with respect to the policy of **undertaxing** millionaires, billionaires, and oil companies that make record profits on high gas prices. Debt and deficits therefore become instances of **revenue neglect.**

It would be useful to return *tax* to its previous positive sense, and marking worthwhile public works and programs with **Your Taxes at Work** again might be a good way to start. Words stressing what you get for taxes include **dues** and **fees. Dues** stresses membership in an institution that is supported by its members. The **dues** pay for what the members get in general. In a health club, "dues" cover general facilities and salaries, maintenance, utilities, and so on. **Fees** cover specific things like yoga lessons. In public life, you might pay "dues" to Friends of the Library and a "fee" for one-day parking in public parks.

Services is a business term, referring to charges made for specific services; you pay only for the services you receive. The business has no moral obligation to the customer, and the customer none to the business. It is just a matter of a market transaction. The term *government services* is therefore misleading because it ignores the moral bond all citizens have to each other, including the moral bond between civil servants and the citizens they serve. The problem with using the term is that it suggests that a private business in the service industry could do the job just as well as the government. It therefore buys into conservative policies of privatization of most government services—that is, most of the moral missions carried out by civil servants in the government for the benefit of the citizenry, not for private profit.

Another problem with speaking of *government services* is that it turns citizens into consumers, which is another step away from the moral mission of government and toward privatization. Citizens are part of their government and have a role in shaping it. Consumers are not part of the businesses they purchase services from and have no say in how those businesses are run or who should run them.

Notice that phrases like *free health care* evoke the same business frame: that health care is a product that can be sold for a price or offered for free. But health care isn't free. It is publicly financed. Calling it *free* buys into the market frame for health care and makes sick and injured people consumers. It makes government a business, and a bad business at that, since good businesses don't give their products away for free. If they do, they run up debts and deficits. It suggests a need for privatization so that real businessmen would run government as a business. This is the Mitt Romney argument.

Democrats speak of realizing *the American Dream* as their goal for all Americans who don't now have the money. *The American Dream* frame is about individuals (a dream, strictly speaking, occurs to a single person asleep) and about what money can buy: a nice home, one or more cars, TVs, a yearly vacation, good health care, a college education, more than enough to eat.

The impulse for Democrats comes from empathy with those who are too poor for such things at present. But at bottom this is a money frame that leaves out progressive values and the answer to the question why you should care about anyone else. It doesn't say what kind of a society you want to live in. It doesn't mention the Public, without which any individual dream would be a nightmare. It leaves out the idea that we're all in this together. The Democrats promoting the American Dream may have this idea, but those who want to get there may not, because progressive moral ideals are not part of the American Dream. We suggest instead the phrase **the American Ideal**, since **ideal** refers to both morality and excellence. And since what are called *government services* are realizations of the Public via forms of protection and empowerment for citizens and businesses, they should be spoken of as such. We suggest naming what the Public carries out **civic tasks** and the agencies carrying them out **task forces**.

This is more than simple renaming. It is a rethinking of what the Public seeks to accomplish and how it does so. A **task** is something that needs to be done (it's not wasteful), that comes with a responsibility (it's not impersonal), that takes work and skill, that is part of a larger enterprise and set of responsibilities, and that can't be done by just anybody. That seems to describe the things that have to be done to protect and empower the public: regulation, education, health care, research, enforcement, building and maintaining public infrastructure, and so on. The term **civic** indicates that these tasks are part of public life, not just a private transaction. A **task force** is not simply people sitting in an office doing their individual jobs. A **task force** is optimally organized to carry out the complex tasks of the Public as an integrated group. Included in this rethinking are not just empathy and responsibility, but also the ethic of excellence. The members of a **task force** have a commitment and a joint responsibility to do their job as well as possible.

The term *spending* implies an outlay of money that drains financial resources. No mention is made of what you get for your money or whether it is needed or worth the expense. The term's lack of specificity suggests arbitrariness. It also suggests that you do a lot of it, with no indication of how worthwhile it is. Conservatives have introduced the term *government spending,* which implies that the money is wasted and the spenders are spendthrifts. Anything necessary or good that happens as a result is not part of the frame, nor are the citizens or businesses that benefit.

Democratic economists use the term *spending* to define money put into the economy, usually targeted to make it grow, as with a **stimulus.** This ignores what the term means to the public. When Democrats use *spending* as economists do they are just helping the conservative agenda to take funding away from public enterprises.

Something similar occurs with the conservative epithet *Obam-*

acare. The term focuses on the proposer of the legislation rather than the people it helps or its moral value or its importance in both the life of individuals and the life of the nation. In recent months, Democrats, including members of the administration, have adopted the word, thus helping the conservative cause.

The Obama administration further obliged by giving the legislation a terrible name, the Affordable Care Act. *Affordable* is disastrous in three ways. First, it places health and life in the commerce frame, using the "health care as product" metaphor. Second, it doesn't place health care in a moral frame, ignoring the moral dimensions of care. This opened the door for conservatives to frame it from their moral perspective as a *government takeover* and to focus on the use of cost-benefit analysis to constrain elder care as *death panels.* Third, the word suggests low quality; what is affordable is not necessarily valuable. Imagine if it had been called **the American Plan.** It would be a lot harder to attack and a pleasure to mention at every opportunity. **The American Plan** is patriotic; it suggests that we're all in this together; and it suggests excellence.

Let us return to the case of *government spending.* What's the alternative? One suggestion is **investment.** Subsidies for sun, wind, water, and soil energy sources would be an **investment** in the future, as would infrastructure building, high-speed rail, and education. All of these are **investments in America.** Maintaining existing programs and financing the debt are not **investments;** they are **maintenance costs.**

Other frames conservatives brought to public discourse, and that many Democrats bought into, are the concepts *deficit, debt,* and *debt ceiling.* As we pointed out earlier, a national budget is not at all like a family budget: as a nation, we owe money mainly to ourselves, can print money, and can borrow it cheaply. We need a frame to say these things and to point out that conservative tax, antiregulation, and subsidy policies are significant causes of the current financial situation. Conservative fiscal policies should be called what they are: **deficit creation policies.** As we mentioned earlier, terms like **revenue neglect** and **undertaxing** can be used to discuss such policies.

The language of the *safety net* has certain disadvantages, which conservatives have taken advantage of in referring to it as a *hammock*. The mental images of the two ideas are similar, but there is a deeper connection that helps promote conservative opinions about social programs. The person falling into the safety net is passive; he or she is not holding up the net, others are. But the reality is that the person who needs Social Security, Medicare, or unemployment compensation has contributed to his or her own security through a lifetime of work. The safety net image leaves out that crucial fact, allowing the hammock image to make sense. You cannot hold up the hammock you are lying in. With both safety nets and hammocks, you depend on other forces. This allows conservatives to suggest that safety nets build dependency and take away the incentive to work.

The safety net metaphor has further metaphorical implications. One *falls downward* into a net, as far down as one can fall. Metaphorically, control is up, loss of control is down, falling is failing, and immoral is down. The implication is that people who rely on social programs are failures who have lost control of their financial lives and are immoral in becoming dependent on others. In conservative religion, falling activates the idea of a fall from grace. All this fits into the conservative moral system for politics—that people are individually responsible for their financial state, that needing money indicates a lack of discipline and incentive, and that financial hardship indicates moral failure. The safety net metaphor buys right into this. Any prior or present efforts are hidden by the metaphor.

Similar issues are raised by words like *entitlements* and *benefits*. It was Ronald Reagan who made *entitlements* a dirty word by taking advantage of what it means: what you are "entitled to." The entitlement frame is distinct from the earning frame. You can be entitled to money without earning it. Conservatives say that all payments should be earned, and no one is simply entitled to anything. The framing allow them to get away with this, when the facts contradict it: the so-called entitlements are largely deferred payments for work done earlier. They are a form of earned income.

But the word *entitlements* doesn't say that. Democrats have adopted a version of the entitlement frame using the implicit concept of the social contract: if you work hard and play by the rules all your working life, you are entitled to a secure old age with medical care, and if you are working and laid off, you are entitled to enough to keep you going until you get your next job. But this is implicit and not in the meaning of *entitlements*.

Something similar happens with the term *benefits*. What are called *benefits* are actually forms of earned income: payments for work done, but in the form of health care, pensions, severance pay, and so on. Benefits and entitlements are largely **deferred pay.** The word *benefits* hides the fact that they are earned income instead of something given to people out of goodwill. Employer-paid health care should be called **worker-earned health care.** The employer isn't giving you health care out of the goodness of his or her heart. You are earning it, partly by working and partly through your loyalty to your employer. Many workers stay on their jobs just to keep their health care coverage. From the employer's perspective, **worker loyalty** benefits business and increases profit because regularly recruiting and training new workers would be costly. The present move to cut benefits is actually a move to cut pay and to avoid paying in full what workers have earned. How can we better express the truths of the situation?

There are two important hidden truths. The first is that workers have paid into Social Security, Medicare, and unemployment insurance, and these are forms of **deferred pay.** The second is subtler. It has to do with the fact that your contribution to society is in most cases not reflected in your income. This is a fact about the way our economy is organized. When corporations view labor as a resource, the natural move is to pay as little as possible for that resource. The result is **workforce dismantling.** There are five kinds of corporate policies to achieve this: union busting so that workers have less bargaining power; using technology to replace workers; organizing work to require the least skill possible; laying off older workers and replacing them with younger ones; and replacing permanent jobs with outsourcing and part-time work.

That is the current reality in our economy. As a result, wages have barely risen over the past three decades. The problem can be seen in the fact, noted earlier, that in 2010, 93 percent of additional income coming to the economy went to the top 1 percent. When labor is a resource, labor is valued as low as possible. It is always on sale.

There are numbers that show this dramatically. Between 2007 and 2011, Standard and Poor's top 500 companies increased their revenue per employee from $378,000 to $420,000.[48] There were no similar increases in wages. Workers are producing more profit for their companies but are not getting paid for it. If they were to get paid for it, there would be less company profit per employee.

In fact these gains were achieved by what is often referred to as "shedding employees," as if workers were extra pounds on an overweight person. These companies make more profit by laying off workers or outsourcing work to countries with cheaper labor. These are considered gains in the efficiency and productivity of the *company*, but they are actually gains in worker efficiency and worker productivity. But because workers are viewed as resources to be used more efficiently by the company, the words *efficiency* and *productivity* make sense from the company's perspective.

The Democratic idea of the **social contract** is an implicit, but never explicitly stated, attempt to remedy this bottom-line perspective. Working as hard as possible over a lifetime, whatever your job or your pay, is a lifetime's worth of contribution to society. And it is not the only one. Being a good citizen, a reliable community member, and a dependable family member are also contributions to society that have little or no correlation with wages but are tremendously important for a stable society, which is an absolute requirement for political freedom, private life, and private business.

When most of the income and assets go to the top 1 percent of society, the contributions to society of the 99 percent are ignored. All of this needs to be in public discourse.

Free market is a conservative term. Democrats should avoid it. The market is, of course, hardly free. It is only relatively free of regulation that protects consumers and workers. The progressive alternative term, **liberal market,** recognizes the market's dependence on the Public and its ethical obligation toward maintaining the Public. The **liberal market** understands the need for regulation, fair taxation, and unions. The **liberal market** is a long-term market, recognizing that short-term greed puts stress on our economy, our environment, and our workforce. Short-term investors looking for the quickest profits put pressure on firms to **dismantle their workforces.**

If there is one expression to avoid above all others in the workplace, it is *human resources*. Once human beings are framed as resources, it follows that their cost should be minimized. The alternative way to frame employees is as **assets** that are valuable to the company. **Assets** go on the positive side of the balance sheet. That is the upside of using this term. The downside is that both *asset* and *resource* language makes employees into economic units, not people.

There is a rift in the Left that goes undiscussed. It arises from reasonable objections to laissez-faire markets and from the absence of a serious discussion of **liberal markets.** If you don't acknowledge or accept the existence of **liberal markets,** then the choice you are left with is to be anticapitalist. *Anticapitalism,* a term used by the far Left, is neither likely to overtake capitalism in the United States nor desirable.

In traditional economic theory, as well as in cold war Hollywood movies, capitalism is pitted against communism, which conservatives and many other Americans don't distinguish from socialism and Marxism. They lump them all together as inherently evil, while believing that capitalism is inherently good. Accepting and discussing **liberal markets** is the antidote to this false dichotomy.

The terms *class warfare* and *redistribution of wealth* originated in a Marxist context. They have been adopted by conservatives as terms of ridicule toward anyone who opposes laissez-faire markets. The assumption is that the failure of communism automatically discredits anyone who speaks of a redistribution of wealth or income redistribution, as many Democrats do. This is the wrong issue for Democrats. The frame of redistribution implies two things. First, it is taking money that people already have and giving it to people who, technically at least, have not earned it themselves. This sounds unfair. Second, it makes the issue one of money only. But it goes way beyond that. The moral concern here is equal empowerment and protection. This is connected to money, but it is not about money per se.

This is also why the phrase *Tax the rich* is misleading. It is not the money per se that is the issue, but the empowerment and protection that the money can buy. Taxing the rich fairly may be a good idea. Great wealth allows control of valuable resources, including political power, something that is hidden by simply calling them *the rich,* as if money alone were the issue. The *Tax the rich* frame involves no progressive values whatsoever.

Conservatives frequently use the Marxist term *class warfare* with regard to people who advocate income redistribution. Some people on the Left have accepted the class warfare frame, trying to turn it around to claim that the rich are conducting class warfare against the poor. This doesn't work for two reasons. First, *class warfare* refers to the poor fighting the rich, not the reverse. Second, the term is strongly associated with its use by Marxists, even if you are not using the term in its Marxist sense. Democrats should avoid the *class warfare* term.

20

Family Freedom

In the strict father family model, the mother is subordinate, a supporter of the father's authority. The father has the final say about sex and reproduction and is the principal breadwinner, protector, and decider. This model maps onto politics in a way that preserves male dominance. Conservative legislation mandating spousal and parental notification for an abortion is one consequence, as is the refusal by the 2012 conservative House of Representatives to renew the Violence Against Women Act. So is the attempt by conservatives in the House to cancel the requirement that health insurance plans provide birth control pills, while allowing any employer who has a religious or moral objection to refuse to pay for birth control pills in insurance coverage. And, of course, so is the constant attempt to make abortion illegal or unfunded or intimidated out of existence.

Led by Democratic women, Democrats are calling all of this the Republican War on Women and using it in fundraising appeals for Democratic candidates. We certainly hope it helps them raise money. The War on Women language has been defended on the grounds that the Republican policies do harm women, and indeed they do. More important, Democrats think they can use this campaign to get independent and even Republican women to vote Democratic. They think the War on Women frame is a winner politically. Yet Rush Limbaugh's response is telling: "Republicans date women, they marry women, they have children with women. They take women to dinner. They buy women diamonds and open car doors for women. Yet there's this Republican war on women, and the Republicans want to actually somehow reach into their purses and grab their birth control pills and take 'em away from 'em. The Democrats actually think that they're going to win with this!"[49]

Limbaugh may well be right to be skeptical. This is the wrong framing strategy. It just isn't believable that the Republican Party, half of which is women, is fighting a war against women. Women who accept the strict father family paradigm and its moral correlates in conservative politics are not going to believe the War on Women metaphor. The metaphor tells women that they have to be militant, that they must organize and fight. Yet women who are naturally nurturant, however strong they may be, may well not want to be militant.

We sincerely hope this campaign, since it is not going to end, succeeds as well as possible. But we would not be surprised if it had little effect in organizing American women who are not already militant on feminist issues. It is important that those involved in the campaign have a realistic understanding of its limits.

We also want to point out that all of these issues concern men as well as women. Remember, 100 percent of all pregnancies are caused by men, and having a child in most instances implies lifelong involvement for the man as well as the woman. Framing pregnancies and abortions as women's issues hides that fact. Additionally, men are the vast majority of culprits in cases of violence against women. We need to get over the idea that these are women's issues. The frame makes women into victims, as does the War on Women frame.

There is a great deal to say about other language issues that deal with family freedom. For instance, the term *pro-life* uses moral language, while *pro-choice* uses consumer language. Moral language always beats consumer language in messages seeking to sway opinion. In addition, by focusing on choice, the liberal language evokes criteria for choosing, a list of supposed pros and cons—as if there were any positive aspects of an unwelcome or forced pregnancy. *Choice* therefore has lots of framing negatives.

For many women the issue of preventing a pregnancy is a matter of liberty, of the freedom to live your life as you want. You can think of it as a **pro-liberty** issue. It is also a matter of having the family that makes sense to you, and so it is a **pro-family** issue, a matter of **family freedom.**

The terms *birth control* and *birth control pills* are disastrous. The real issue is **pregnancy prevention.** The word *birth* has a frame that includes a fully formed baby and a woman giving birth, often the happiest moment of her life. This, however, has nothing to do with men and women avoiding an unwelcome pregnancy.

Similarly, the term *abortion* has misleading properties. When we speak of "aborting a mission," we are referring to a mission that was intentional and planned, for which the original idea was to bring it to an end state. What happens with an unwelcome pregnancy is nothing like this. The pregnancy was not intentional, was not planned, and there was never any intention of bringing it to an end state. Rather what is desired is **development prevention,** keeping any development from happening. Development can be prevented at many stages, from blastocyst to embryo, from embryo to fetus, from fetus to a not fully formed human or unviable human (one that can't live outside the womb). The earlier the development prevention, the better for the woman.

The term *partial birth abortion* was invented by a conservative-language expert. The image is grisly, and that was the point. But no such thing exists. The medical condition it is supposed to represent is one where a potential child cannot survive, either because it has no brain or because of some other equally awful condition. And usually the mother's life is at risk. This has nothing to do with giving birth or with the usual reasons for **preventing development.**

When a couple is trying to have a child, they think of the child as it will be born after it has developed in the womb and the mother has given birth successfully. At that stage, the appropriate term is certainly *baby*. But since they are thinking ahead to the stage after birth, they usually refer to the earlier stages with the same word. That is perfectly natural. What is not perfectly natural is using the same term in the case of **development prevention**. There are appropriate terms for whatever the stage is: **blastocyst, embryo,** or **fetus** in almost all cases.

The term *mother* comes with several frames that most commonly fit together. In the birth frame, the woman who gives birth to the baby is the mother. In the nurturance frame, the woman who raises the baby is the mother. In the marriage frame, the woman married to the child's father is the mother. And in the genetic frame, the woman that provides half of the gene pool of the child is the mother. In the typical case, these frames all come together. But when they do not, we get special terms like *birth mother, biological mother, stepmother,* and *foster mother*.

In all these cases, however, the baby has to have been born for there to be a mother. Women who seek development prevention ought to be referred to as **women,** not *mothers*. Yet in conservative political discourse, a woman who has at least a fertilized egg is called a *mother*. This unusual use of language has a political purpose. It is a means of shaming a woman who wants to prevent development on the grounds that she is already a mother. In the case of development prevention, a mother can be charged with baby killing. This is a political use of language that can have terrifying effects.

21

Social Darwinism

On April 3, 2012, when President Obama referred to an extreme conservative budget as "thinly veiled Social Darwinism,"[50] the media went wild trying to explain what he meant. As we shall see, he got it right. But to understand the reference, we need to know the difference between real Darwinism and social Darwinism. This is tricky, and Democrats sometimes get it wrong.

The word *Darwinian* has two very different meanings. It can refer simply to Darwin's theory of evolution, and it can refer to the false account of Darwin's theory as interpreted by the conservatives of Darwin's time, which has been repeated so often as to come into public discourse: "relating to, or being a competitive environment or situation in which only the fittest persons or organizations prosper." Here *fittest* refers to individual strength. This is social Darwinism, popularized by Herbert Spencer and other conservatives of Darwin's day. But in Darwin's actual theory, the word *fittest* meant fitting best into an ecological niche. The species that survived best fit their niches.

Darwin personally contested the conservative interpretation of his theory, here in *The Origin of Species*: "I use this term [*struggle for existence*] in a large and metaphorical sense including dependence of one being upon another, and including (which is more important) not only the life of the individual, but success in leaving progeny. Two canine animals, in times of dearth, may be truly said to struggle with each other, which shall get food and life. But a plant on the edge of a desert is said to struggle for life against the drought, though more properly it should be said to be dependent on the moisture."[51]

Darwin explicitly described empathy and cooperation, not competition, as natural traits of humans and animals and as central to the survival of animal species: "We are impelled to relieve the sufferings of another, in order that our own painful feelings may be at the same time relieved." Darwin argued that empathy is crucial to species survival: "In however complex a manner this feeling may have originated, as it is one of high importance to all those animals which aid and defend one another, it will have been increased through natural selection; for those communities, which included the greatest number of the most sympathetic members, would flourish best, and rear the greatest number of offspring."

Darwin not only believed empathy was key to species survival, but saw in it the greatest social virtue: "As man advances in civilization, and small tribes are united into larger communities, the simplest reason would tell each individual that he ought to extend his social instincts and sympathies to all members of the same nation, though personally unknown to him. This point being once reached, there is only an artificial barrier to prevent his sympathies extending to the men of all nations and races."

In short, real Darwinian values accord with progressive Democratic values, and Democrats should say so. Democrats should be speaking of **Darwinian empathy, Darwinian cooperation,** and **Darwinian social cohesion.** As Darwin observed, we evolved to have empathy for and be cooperative with others. Empathy and taking responsibility to act on it have allowed species to survive, and it allows societies to survive and thrive.

President Obama has sometimes sounded a lot like Darwin. In 2008 he spoke repeatedly of the "empathy deficit" in America. In an interview on April 1, 2008, on NBC's *Today* show, when Ann

Curry asked, "Best thing your mom ever taught you?," Obama responded, "Empathy. Making sure that you can see the world through somebody else's eyes, stand in their shoes. I think that's the basis for kindness and compassion." And here is Obama in an interview on the television show *Anderson Cooper 360* on March 19, 2008: "The core of patriotism [is] . . . are we caring for each other? Are we upholding the values of our founders? Are we willing to sacrifice on behalf of future generations?"

Darwin noted that empathy created social unity, both in animals and in human beings. In modern neuroscience, mirror neuron systems in both monkeys and humans display the mechanism of this most vital of evolutionary inheritances. Obama has understood this, as well as the fact that extreme conservatives, for over a century, have tried to twist Darwin to their own purposes with social Darwinism, which is not a form of Darwinism at all. It is a form of extreme conservative morality, of individuals always in competition in a you're-on-your-own society. Why would conservatives want this (mis)interpretation of Darwinism? In order to make their social views seem natural, that competition and greed are a natural part of who we are. The only way to seriously counter this over the long run is to regularly quote the real Darwin and point out the difference.

The problem here is that the theme of competition runs so deep in American culture, politics, and economics that even Democrats base major policies on it. Equality is defined as fairness of competition, as when the *level playing field* metaphor is invoked in discussions of race, gender, and sexual preference. Education is defined as promoting a higher level of competition for well-paying jobs. Energy policy is seen as seeking competition between clean and dirty energy sources.

Obama's Race to the Top initiative applies the competition metaphor to education on many levels. The competition is, first of all, among the states competing for extra education funding. Then public schools compete, both with each other and with charter schools, as "failing schools" are punished, often with elimination. Education itself becomes competition, where learning is defined as winning in the testing competition. And teaching becomes a competition between teachers to see who is best at teaching competition, with the prize of merit pay and the threat of getting fired. Progressive educators are deeply disturbed by Race to the Top because it abandons the progressive values of critical thinking, self-realization, multiple intelligences, empathy, and cooperation. If Obama has liberal values, where are they in Race to the Top?

In his Father's Day speech in 2008, Obama talked about the responsibility of parents for their children's education and about instilling in children not only a sense of responsibility and empathy but also a sense of excellence. He has also talked repeatedly about fairness, about everyone having an equal chance in society. As a sports fan and basketball player, he recognizes the enormous role that competition plays in American society and the fact that competition can hone one's skills and contribute to excellence. We suspect that President Obama views Race to the Top from this perspective. Tests are forms of competition. Learning to do well on tests hones one's skill. High grades testify to excellence. Objective tests are fair and give everyone an equal chance to do well. This is a liberal version of competition. But this perspective does not change the fact that Race to the Top is an inherently conservative model of education.

Notice that Race to the Top also involves the metaphor *more is up* (and therefore *better*)—more intelligence, more money, more prestige, more discipline, and more character. This coincides with usages like *upper, middle,* and *lower classes.* Talking about the middle class, as Obama does regularly, activates the frame of upper and lower, as does the phrase *upward mobility.* Even the denial of the idea that prosperity *trickles down from the top* activates this frame. So too does the implication that the poor are at the bottom. Much more is being said here than one would notice at first glance. Moral is up. Power is up. Functionality is up. The divine is up. All these metaphors are regularly invoked when you reason about people in terms of verticality.

Verticality metaphors are important politically because they directly play into the hands of conservative morality. When *more is up* and *moral is up* are bound together, people understand that *the rich are better.* Binding together *more is up* and *control is up* leads to an inference that those with more resources should naturally have more control over society. Binding *more is up* with *The divine is up* leads to the inference that *the rich are closer to God.* Finally, binding *more is up* with *functionality is up* suggests that those with high positions contribute more to the functioning of society and our economy. This makes managerial bonuses and merit pay perfectly natural phenomena.

A special case is *the top 1 percent.* The expression says nice things about the folks at the top. Wouldn't you like to be at the top? Not just rich, but moral, in control, and closer to God? Interestingly, neither President Obama nor his conservative opponents want to mention a top 1 percent fact: that 93 percent of the additional income that entered the economy in 2010 went to the top 1 percent. The market as it is now is a **1 percent market.**

That is the real point. There will always be a richest 1 percent. The issue is the *degree* of disparity in wealth and power. A market that disproportionately robs the 99 percent and rewards 1 percent should be called a **1 percent market.** Not a free market. Not a laissez-faire market. A **1 percent market.**

AFTERWORD

It is very difficult to introduce new ideas and new language. Don't expect them to work immediately. Conservatives have an advantage because the ideas they use were introduced into public discourse by earlier conservatives over three or more decades. Adding new language when the related fundamental ideas are in place is relatively easy, but introducing new ideas and new language at the same time—and adding lots of them—is hard.

It takes a lot of repetition by a lot of people to change public discourse in any significant way. They have done it. You can do it.

NOTES

A Note About This Book

1 Andrea Rock, *The Mind at Night* (Basic Books, 2005).

2 George Lakoff, "What Orwell Didn't Know about the Brain, the Mind, and Language," in András Szántó, ed., *What Orwell Didn't Know: Propaganda and the New Face of American Politics* (Public Affairs, 2007), 67–74; Paula Niedenthal, Lawrence Barsalou, Piotr Winkielman, Silvia Krauth-Gruber, and François Ric, "Embodiment in Attitude, Social Perception and Emotion," *Personality and Social Psychology Review* 9 (2005): 184–211; Paul Thibodeau and Lera Boroditsky, "Metaphors We Think With: The Role of Metaphor in Reasoning," *PLoS ONE* 6, no. 2 (2011); Lawrence Barsalou, "Grounded Cognition," *Annual Review of Psychology* 59 (2008): 617–45.

3 Charles Fillmore, "An Alternative to Checklist Theories in Meaning," *Proceedings of the First Annual Meeting of the Berkeley Linguistics Society,* February 1975, 123–31, online; Charles Fillmore, "Frame Semantics," in Linguistic Society of Korea, ed., *Linguistics in the Morning Calm* (Hanshin, 1985), 111–38; George Lakoff and Mark Johnson, *Metaphors We Live By* (University of Chicago Press, 1980); Raymond Gibbs, "Why Many Concepts Are Metaphorical," *Cognition* 61 (1996): 309–19; Jerome Feldman, *From Molecule to Metaphor: A Neural Theory of Language* (MIT Press, 2006).

4 Simon Lacey, Randall Stilla, and Krish Sathian, "Metaphorically Feeling: Comprehending Textural Metaphors Activates Somatosensory Cortex," *Brain and Language* 120, no. 3 (2012): 416–21; Dan Jones, "Moral Psychology: The Depth of Disgust," *Nature* 447 (2007): 768–71.

Chapter 1

5 Martin Lankheet, "Unraveling Adaptation and Mutual Inhibition in Perceptual Rivalry," *Journal of Vision* 6, no. 4 (2006): 304–10.

6 Walter Bryce Gallie, "Essentially Contested Concepts," *Proceedings of the Aristotelian Society* 56 (1956): 167–98.

135

NOTES

Chapter 4

7 Stanislas Dehaene, *Reading in the Brain: The Science and Evolution of a Human Invention* (Viking, 2009); Antonio Damasio, "The Brain Binds Entities and Events by Multiregional Activation from Convergence Zones," *Neural Computation* 1, no. 1 (1989): 123–32; Antonio Damasio and Hanna Damasio, "Cortical Systems for Retrieval of Concrete Knowledge: The Convergence Zone Framework," in Christof Koch and Joel Davis, eds., *Large-Scale Neuronal Theories of the Brain* (MIT Press, 1995), 61–74.

Chapter 5

8 Public Citizen, "Myths and Lies about Single Payer," March 2012.

9 Thibodeau and Boroditsky, "Metaphors We Think With."

10 Media Matters, "CNN's Dana Loesch: Al Gore's Climate-Change Documentary Was 'The Same Level of Propaganda' as Leni Riefenstahl's Films," February 2, 2012, http://mediamatters.org/mmtv/201202020004.

11 Eleanor Rosch, Carolyn Mervis, Wayne Gray, David Johnson, and Penny Boyes-Braem, "Basic Objects in Natural Categories," *Cognitive Psychology* 8, no. 3 (1976): 382–439.

Chapter 7

12 Laurence Steinberg, Julie Elmen, and Nina Mounts, "Authoritative Parenting, Psychosocial Maturity, and Academic Success among Adolescents," *Child Development* 60, no. 6 (1989): 1424–36; Laurence Steinberg, Susie Lamborn, Sanford Dornbusch, and Nancy Darling, "Impact of Parenting Practices on Adolescent Achievement: Authoritative Parenting, School Involvement, and Encouragement to Succeed," *Child Development* 63, no. 5 (1992): 1266–81; Quing Zhou, Nancy Eisenberg, Yun Wang, and Mark Reiser, "Chinese Children's Effortful Control and Dispositional Anger/Frustration: Relations to Parenting Styles and Children's Social Functioning," *Developmental Psychology* 40, no. 3 (2004): 352–66; Maja Dekovic and Jan Janssens, "Parents' Child-rearing Style and Child's Sociometric Status," *Developmental Psychology* 28, no. 5 (1992): 925–32; Tanja Rothrauff, Teresa Cooney, and Jeong Shin An, "Remembered Parenting Styles and Adjustment in Middle and Late Adulthood," *Journals of Gerontology* 64, no. 1 (2009): 137–46; Philip Greven, *Spare the Child* (New York: Alfred A. Knopf, 1991).

Chapter 8

13 "Shaheen Amendment to Restore Abortion Coverage for Military Rape Victims Bypassed in Senate, *Huffington Post,* December 1, 2011.

14 "Women in Texas Losing Options for Health Care in Abortion Fight," *New York Times,* March 7, 2012.

15 "Virginia's Proposed Ultrasound Law Is an Abomination," *Slate,* February 16, 2012.

16 "Georgia's Terry England: Women Should Carry Dead Babies to Term," *Daily Kos,* March 20, 2012.

17 Kate Randall, "U.S. Women Charged with Murder Following Miscarriage," World Socialist Web Site, July 6, 2011.

18 United Nations, The Universal Declaration of Human Rights, http://www.un.org/en/documents/udhr/.

Chapter 10

19 Lucy Madison, "Elizabeth Warren: 'There Is Nobody in This Country Who Got Rich on His Own,'" CBS News, September 22, 2011, http://www.cbsnews.com/8301-503544_162-20110042-503544.html.

Chapter 11

20 "The Rich Get Even Richer," *New York Times,* March 26, 2012.

Chapter 12

21 Cynthia S. Mutryn, "Psychosocial Impact of Cesarean Section on the Family: A Literature Review," *Social Science & Medicine* 37, no. 10 (1993): 1271–81.

Chapter 13

22 Outsourcing is mainly done to save money, typically by corporations as means of increasing profits or by Republican governments to cut spending. Money is saved by using cheap labor abroad and/or by not being responsible for benefits and pensions. Contracting out is commonplace in government, as when the defense department contracts out the development of missiles and fighter planes to companies with considerable expertise that the government doesn't have or doesn't see any reason to develop. Private industry contracts out for the same reason.

23 Thomas Gammel Toft-Hansen, "Can Privatization Kill?," *New York Times,* April 1, 2012.

24 Dana Priest, *Top Secret America: The Rise of the New American Security State* (Little, Brown, 2011).

25 Donald Rumsfeld, "The Future of Iraq," lecture, Johns Hopkins Paul H. Nitze School of Advanced International Studies, May 12, 2005.

26 "C.I.A. Sought Blackwater's Help to Kill Jihadists," *New York Times,* August 19, 2009.

27 Priest, *Top Secret America.*

28 Liz Brown and Eric Gutstein, "The Charter Difference: A Comparison of Chicago Charter and Neighborhood High Schools." Collaborative for Equity and Justice in Education, University of Illinois, Chicago, 2009, http://www.uic.edu/educ/ceje/articles/CharterDifference.pdf.

29 Mike Barrett, "Bottled Water Regulation," Natural Society, 2001, http://naturalsociety.com/bottled-water-regulation-regulated-less-than-tap-water/.

30 Paul Healy and Krishna Palepu, "The Fall of Enron," *Journal of Economic Perspectives* 17, no. 2 (2003): 15.

Chapter 16

31 Giacomo Rizzolatti, Luciano Fadiga, Vittorio Gallese, and Leonardo Fogassi, "Research Report: Premotor Cortex and the Recognition of Motor Actions, *Cognitive Brain Research* 3, no. 2 (1996): 131–41; Vittorio Gallese, Luciano Fadiga, Leonardo Fogassi, and Giacomo Rizzolatti, "Action Recognition in the Premotor Cortex," *Brain* 119, no. 2 (1996): 593–609.

32 "City-Dwelling Investors Got $394M in Farm Subsidies Last Year," Alter Net, June 27, 2011, http://www.alternet.org/economy/151445/city-dwelling_investors_got_$394m_in_farm_subsidies_last_year/.

33 "If You Eat, You Need to Know," Take Part, August 6, 2011, http://www.takepart.com/article/2011/08/04/if-you-eat-you-need-know-5-facts-about-farm-bill.

34 Alisha Coleman-Jensen, Mark Nord, Margaret Andrews, and Steven Carlson, "Household Food Security in the United States in 2010," U.S. Department of Agriculture, Economic Research Service, http://www.ers.usda.gov/Publications/ERR125/.

35 Daniel Imhoff, *Food Fight: The Citizen's Guide to the Next Food and Farm Bill*, 2nd edition (Watershed Media, 2012).

36 Ibid.

37 "Big Food vs. Big Insurance," *New York Times*, September 10, 2009.

38 "Toxic Waste Use as Fertilizer on Farms Reported," *Los Angeles Times*, July 7, 1997; Matthew Shaffer, "Waste Lands: The Threat of Toxic Fertilizers," California Public Interest Research Group Charitable Trust, 2001, online.

39 Imhoff, *Food Fight*.

Chapter 17

40 An example in English is the transitive verb "break" indicating the directly causal act that leaves something broken.

41 "The Keystone XL Pipeline Fails America," *Daily Kos*, February 25, 2012.

42 Ted Turner, "Stop Keystone Pipeline Before It's Too Late," CNN Opinion, February 24, 2012, http://www.cnn.com/2012/02/22/opinion/turner-keystone-pipeline/index.html.

43 Anthony Swift, "The Keystone XL Tar Sands Pipeline Leak Detection System Would Have Likely Missed the 63,000 Gallon Norman Wells Pipeline Spill," Natural Resources Defense Council, June 10, 2011, http://switchboard.nrdc.org/blogs/aswift/the_keystone_xl_tar_sands_pipe.html.

44 Anthony Swift, "New Report: Keystone XL Will Undermine U.S. Energy Security," Natural Resources Defense Council, January 18, 2012, http://switchboard.nrdc.org/blogs/aswift/new_report_keystone_xl_will_un.html.

45 Mitt Romney on the *Charlie Sykes Show*, March 22, 2012.

46 "Mitt Romney's Illinois Victory Speech," Real Clear Politics, March 20, 2012, http://www.realclearpolitics.com/articles/2012/03/20/mitt_romneys_illinois_victory_speech_113565.html.

Chapter 18
47 "Survey Research Illuminating American Public Opinion on Climate and Energy," Stanford Woods Institute for the Environment, http://woods.stanford.edu/research/surveys.html.

Chapter 19
48 "The Two Economies," *New York Times,* April 9, 2012.

Chapter 20
49 "The War on Women Didn't Work," *The Rush Limbaugh Show,* March 15, 2012. http://www.rushlimbaugh.com/daily/2012/03/15/the_war_on_women_didn_t_work.

Chapter 21
50 "Obama: Ryan Budget Thinly Veiled 'Darwinism,'" CBN.com, April 3, 2012, http://www.cbn.com/cbnnews/politics/2012/April/Obama-Ryan-Budget-Thinly-Veiled-Darwanism/.
51 Online Variorum of Darwin's *Origen of Species*: fourth British edition (1866), page 73.

ACKNOWLEDGMENTS

Important ideas came from conversations with Kathleen Frumkin, Glenn Smith, Ken Cook, Michael Pollan, and Daniel Kammen.

ABOUT THE AUTHORS

George Lakoff is Goldman Distinguished Professor of Cognitive Science and Linguistics at the University of California, Berkeley. He is the author of the *New York Times* bestseller *Don't Think of an Elephant! Know your Values and Frame the Debate* and is America's leading expert on the framing of political ideas.

Elisabeth Wehling is a political strategist, author, and journalist. She is doing research in linguistics at the University of California, Berkeley, on how politics is understood in both the United States and Europe.